Act Three

Edited by David Self
and Ray Speakman

To Ruari,

Best wishes,

Geoff.

Hutchinson of London

Contents

Hutchinson & Co. (Publishers) Ltd
3 Fitzroy Square, London W1P 6JD

London Melbourne Sydney Auckland
Wellington Johannesburg and agencies
throughout the world

First published 1979

This selection and notes © David Self and Ray Speakman 1979

Set in IBM Press Roman

Printed in Great Britain by litho at The Anchor Press Ltd
and bound by Wm Brendon & Son Ltd, both of
Tiptree, Essex

ISBN 0 09 136961 4

Introduction

Of the four new plays published for the first time in this collection, *Annie Kenney* was written for a television drama series
about the Suffragette Movement called *Shoulder to Shoulder*,
while the other three plays were written for the stage.

The first of these, *Some Enchanted Evening*, is by the Glasgow-
born playwright, C.P. Taylor, who was for several years Literary
Associate at the University Theatre, Newcastle-upon-Tyne. His
play is very firmly set in Newcastle – besides many references to
parts of the city and its suburbs, he brings in a number of local
jokes about Gateshead (just across the River Tyne), about local
television programmes, and about such things as a locally brewed
beer known as Federation.

Indeed, the play is set in a type of social (or drinking) club
that is typical of the North-east, and any production of the play
should make the most of this, perhaps to the extent of inviting
the audience to join in a bingo session during the interval and of
having a live group play before and after the play, as well as at
the points shown in the script. (NB It would be possible to dis-
pense with an actual group and to rely on records, however.)

Some Enchanted Evening is about Peter, a young man in his
twenties who is a packer in Wills's cigarette factory just outside
Newcastle. The play opens with him sitting in the club, remember-
ing how he was once sitting there, drinking, when he was joined
by a girl who was thinking of committing suicide. As he remem-
bers the incident, the girl in question enters and the scene is

acted out in front of us in a kind of 'flashback'; and in turn it reminds Peter of how he once attempted suicide by jumping from the George V bridge, the arched suspension bridge that crosses the Tyne and connects Newcastle with Gateshead.

Climbing up on a chair, he thinks himself back on the bridge and we see the various characters he then encounters: the passers-by, a policeman almost totally preoccupied with his own problems, a Samaritan, his former girlfriend Sue, his parents, and a television reporter. In flashbacks within the main flashback, we see how Sue courted Peter, until she talked him into an engagement; and we also see something of Peter's home life with his parents.

Act 2 opens with the girl in the club showing a lot of interest in Peter: this reminds him of how Sue pursued him, and so we move into another sequence of flashbacks – how she nagged at him to get fit, eventually making him go to a trainer in a gymnasium; and also how she tried to make him get a 'better' job (driving a van for Securicor). We discover that Peter's mother became jealous of Sue, and that the two women (mother and girlfriend) started a kind of war for 'possession' of Peter. His mother's eventual victory and his rejection of Sue only made him 'bloody sick', and it was this that drove him to his attempted suicide. So the flashbacks-within-the-main-flashback catch up with the original one and we are back with Peter on the bridge. He survives his 'attempt' (in fact he falls rather than jumps), and the play ends with him in the club with the lass – a stranger he has met (in the words of the song) 'Some enchanted evening . . . across a crowded room'.

Though the play may sound very complicated, it is beautifully constructed. Like a Chinese puzzle, the flashbacks nestle neatly inside each other to form a script which is equally appealing as a play to read in class or to stage. (Indeed it is a script which would also be admirably suited to radio or even television.)

Most of all it is a very funny comedy, a play we can sit back and enjoy. Many will find it an appealing mixture of humorous exaggeration, wit and farce, made all the funnier by being punctuated by Peter's endearing asides to the audience. Underneath the music-hall laughter however, there is much honesty and some seriousness. *Some Enchanted Evening* deals perceptively with the pressures of young adulthood, of 'leaving the nest', of job expectations and of courtship. It may seem to be just a picture of Tyneside: in fact it will speak directly and provocatively to young people from any area.

So too will Tom Hadaway's *The Filleting Machine*. This also takes place on Tyneside, but is set in the living room of a council house on a large estate in North Shields. It is the home of a large family — there are six children altogether, the eldest of whom is Davy, soon to leave school. Having got his O-levels, Davy has the chance of a job in the Town Clerk's office. His mother is delighted about this: she sees it as Davy's escape route from their present way of life. An office job represents security, respectability and opportunity. To Davy, an office job is not a proper job, but just "sittin' pretendin' ti be doin' summick important . . . might as well be skule"; and (unknown to his parents) he has accepted a job on the fish quay. Money is good on the quay and there are other 'perks' (the chance to have a 'fiddle') all of which is attractive to Davy, as is the open-air life. His mother still tries to persuade him not to take a dead-end job but to use his education: "Don't let yourself down Davy, an' don't let me down," she says.

Davy's father comes home after work and, also, a fairly heavy drinking bout. In the niggling and argument that follows, it emerges that he is all in favour of Davy working, like him, on the fish quay, filleting the newly landed fish. A worse-than-usual row develops, Davy is caught between divided loyalties and tells his parents he has accepted the job on the quay, at £8 a week more than he would have got in the office. He also reveals, without being aware of the implications, that a filleting machine is being installed — a machine that will render his father redundant. Confirmation of this fact soon comes, Da storms out, and the play closes with Ma reading her eldest daughter's school report which says she shows considerable aptitude for music, and dreaming that perhaps the next of her children might have the chance to 'escape'.

Life on the Ridges estate is rough and Tom Hadaway does not shrink from presenting it realistically. The language is raw but always convincing, as are the characters and their attitudes. Da accepts the situation he finds himself in and has settled for a relatively easy life, content to escape in drink. Ma never closes her mind to what might be, she is the striver, prepared to sacrifice immediate pleasure for long-term betterment. Davy is forced to choose between the two courses and must inevitably displease one parent. Ironically his acceptance of work as what will prove to be a machine-minder pleases neither, but presumably his earnings will be both welcome and necessary for the family.

Some may find the dialect of the play difficult — it is certainly a script that will repay rehearsal before being read aloud, even informally. However, because it is such an accurate picture of an actual locality, it seems wrong to modify the script and it is hoped that the clever transliteration of the Geordie dialect will lead to language work on this and other accents and dialects. While the setting is highly localized, no one can dispute the universality and relevance of the themes and problems that are explored within the play.

If *The Filleting Machine* is socially and geographically realistic then *Annie Kenney* is historically so. All the leading characters are real, as are the events that are chronicled.

Before this century, women had few rights. They were treated by the law as being inferior to men; educational opportunities for girls were less than those for boys; women were paid less than men (even for comparable jobs); and they could not vote at elections. Nor did women have any real chance of success in public life.

Some progress towards women's rights was made during the nineteenth century (e.g. the Married Women's Property Acts which gave women the right to own property and to give it to whom they wished), but the vote remained a long way off.

The leader of the 'Votes-for-Women' movement was Mrs Emmeline Pankhurst, together with her daughters Christabel and Sylvia. In October 1903, at her house in Manchester, Mrs Pankhurst founded the Women's Social and Political Union (WSPU) with the aim of winning votes for women.

This is how she described the beginnings of the movement in a book called *My Own Story:*

We did not begin to fight, however, until we had given the new Government every chance to give us the pledge we wanted. . . . On December 21 [1905] a great meeting was held in the Royal Albert Hall, London, where Sir Henry, surrounded by his cabinet, made his first utterance as Prime Minister. Previous to the meeting we wrote to Sir Henry and asked him, in the name of the Women's Social and Political Union, whether the Liberal Government would give women the vote. . . .

Of course Sir Henry Campbell-Bannerman returned no reply, nor did his speech contain any allusion to women's suffrage. So, at the conclusion, Annie Kenney, whom we had smuggled into the hall in disguise, whipped out her little white calico banner, and called out in her clear, sweet voice: 'Will the Liberal Government give women the vote?'

At the same moment Teresa Billington let drop from a seat directly above the platform a huge banner with the words: Will the Liberal Government give justice to working women?' Just for a moment there was gasping silence, the people waiting to see what the Cabinet Ministers would do. They did nothing. Then, in the middle of uproar and conflicting shouts, the women were seized and flung out of the hall.

This was the beginning of a campaign the like of which was never known in England, or, for that matter in any other country . . . . We attended every meeting addressed by Mr Churchill. We heckled him unmercifully; we spoiled his best points by flinging back such obvious retorts that the crowds roared with laughter . . . .

What good did it do? We have often been asked that question . . . .

For one thing, our heckling campaign made women's suffrage a matter of news – it had never been that before. Now the newspapers were full of us.

On February 19, 1906, occurred the first suffrage procession in London. I think there were between three and four hundred women in that procession, poor working women from the East End, for the most part, leading the way in which numberless women of every rank were afterwards to follow. My eyes were misty with tears as I saw them, standing in line, holding the simple banners which my daughter Sylvia had decorated, waiting for the word of command. Of course our procession attracted a large crowd of intensely amused spectators. . . . Those women had followed me to the House of Commons. They had defied the police. They were awake at last . . . .

It is against the background of these events that Alan Plater has set his moving and precisely written story of the Suffragette movement and of Annie Kenney's part in it.

Rather different from many of the other leading figures, Annie Kenney came from a working-class home while the Pankhursts were distinctly middle class in outlook. (Some have suggested that the Pankhursts would have been content with votes for a small number of rich women. Certainly the new Labour Party under its leader, Keir Hardie, did not fully support the aims of the WSPU).

In a succession of well-selected and well-constructed scenes, Plater shows us the growth of the movement (slightly dotty in some of its eccentric enthusiasms) and of Annie herself, as she grows in political and social awareness to become a modest and likeable heroine. Unlike many of the central characters in the other plays in this collection there is nothing resigned about Annie – she is a fighter and is never content to accept a situation without questioning its rights and wrongs. Convinced that action will succeed, she battles on with confidence and is rewarded with success. Just as she is very obviously like her own mother, so she would gladden the heart of Davy's Ma in *The Filleting Machine*. She is prepared to strive.

Annie Kenney is an inspiring play, and one that is never mawkish. There is no false sentiment – the pathos is always tempered with humour; and it is an excellent example of a well-made television play.

While Alan Plater's play may be a hymn of praise to commitment and involvement, *Here Comes the Sun* is apparently purely escapist.

Set on the patio of a cheap tourist hotel in southern Spain, it chronicles the package tour holiday of a group of factory girls from Hull. Arriving full of excitement at the prospect of letting their hair down on a romantic, sun-drenched Mediterranean holiday, they begin to discover the differences between the illusion and the reality, and we discover that behind the jokes and the banter there is real agony, boredom and violence. Many of the characters have unhappy home lives and their work is monotonous. The holiday represented an escape – but only a temporary one, hence the high spirits in the early scenes, and the determination (at all costs) to have a good time. Though we don't see the English boys in the same kind of close up as we see the girls, the implication is that their drinking and violence is a similar kind of escape or release of frustration.

In addition to the young holidaymakers we are shown the local hotel workers and a few English people who have settled in the town to make an easy living off the tourists – notably Rick who is escaping from a rather murky past and Rod who is playing with a group.

On the one hand, *Here Comes the Sun* may seem just an indulgent comic romp. In fact, behind the often savage humour, it is a serious and pessimistic play which raises a number of important questions about the quality of life and what we can expect of it. However, while it may pose questions (e.g. about the causes of boredom and violence), like many of Barry Keeffe's realistic and highly dramatic plays, it does not set out to provide any answers. Indeed it almost suggests there are no answers, that there is no hope.

This is not to denigrate its value as a play: the author's philosophy is obviously thought-provoking, as are many of the points he raises. Indeed, it is hoped that, like all the plays in this collection, it will sustain much thoughtful discussion as well as being entertaining to read and to perform.

Notes on Presentation

Reading

Even the most informal calssroom reading of a playscript is helped by rehearsal. Remember, not even the experienced professional actor is happy to 'sight-read', but usually prefers to have had the chance at least to look over his part before a first reading in front of his colleagues. So, once a play has been cast, those who will be reading should be given the chance to look over their lines, to make sure they know where they 'enter' and 'exit', that they know when to pause, when to 'come in quickly' at the end of the previous speech; indeed, that they appreciate the mood, etc., of their character at any given moment.

Note that (especially in the case of a play with small cast like *The Filleting Machine*) it is possible for a class to break up into small groups, and for each group to rehearse its own interpretation of the play, before one group 'presents' its reading to the whole class.

Note too that it is much easier to read to a class from the front of a traditional classroom, and from a standing position or a position where you can be seen by your 'audience'. In particular, (because of Peter's asides) *Some Enchanted Evening* positively asks to be read to an audience in this way.

In preparing the scripts for inclusion in this book, we have modified some of the stage directions, and rewritten the camera directions in *Annie Kenney*, so that when the plays are being read aloud these directions (along with the scene titles) can be read aloud by an 'announcer'. In a classroom presentation, it might be helpful if he or she were in view of the 'audience' but away from the acting area.

Note that provided these directions are read sympathetically, a television play like *Annie Kenney* will read as fluently in the classroom as will a stage play; but it should not be forgotten that (like any good television play) it was conceived in visual terms, and it will be fruitful to discuss (as the original director must have done) where and how each scene should be 'shot' to realize the author's intention. Indeed, as has been suggested, the juxta-position of television and stage playscripts in this collection could lead to a study of the differing natures, possibilities, limitations and constructions of such plays.

Staging
The three stage plays in this collection are all relatively straight-forward to stage.

Some Enchanted Evening is set in a social club in Newcastle-upon-Tyne, with flashbacks to scenes in various places around that city. Note that the George V bridge across the Tyne is suggested simply by Peter climbing on a chair, and the other scenes are all created by the dialogue and action. There is little need to point up the flashbacks by changing the lighting: we are always in the club, where Peter is telling and re-enacting a story for us, the audience. There is no need to pretend that we actually are on the bridge, the quayside or in his home. The atmosphere of the club could extend to the auditorium, as has been suggested, with, for example, an actual bingo session run during the interval of the play.

The Filleting Machine needs one realistic set: a council house living room. Care should be taken to see that the set is 'dressed' convincingly — a small room in which a large family lives is likely to be fairly cluttered.

Here Comes the Sun requires one set that suggests the patio of a cheap Spanish hotel. Note that several of the scenes (especially the disco ones) require far more holidaymakers to be present than are named in the cast.

Because *Annie Kenney* is a television script and requires a variety of indoor and outdoor locations, it will prove hard to present it on stage realistically (without major adaptation). It will work successfully, however, if it is given a stylized production either in the round or on an almost empty stage. Specially taken 35 mm slides, projected scenery or captions can announce location to an audience, and the use of sound effects can be an effective substitute for scenery (especially in outdoor scenes such as those at the fairground or railway station). Other exterior scenes could be created entirely by the use of slides and taped voices and sound effects. Sound effects can also be used to suggest the presence of large crowds at meetings, etc. Costumes and hand-held props can do much to replace scenery. In indoor scenes, the use of stage scenery should be severely restricted so as to preserve fluency and speed of staging. Part of the success of any television play lies in the fact that it can cut from one scene to another, and in a stage performance of a television play, lighting changes must be used to effect such 'jump-cuts' and to make us believe the acting area now represents a different location.

The following is a checklist of the various settings:

Rooms
The Kenney living room (one scene)
The Pankhurst sitting room at Nelson Street (three scenes)
The prison visitors' room (two scenes)
Sylvia's studio (nine scenes)
Keir Hardie's flat (six scenes)
The Pethick Lawrence apartment (two scenes)
A café (one scene)

Halls, etc:
The Co-op Hall (two scenes)

The Free Trade Hall (one scene)
A magistrates court (one scene)
Caxton Hall (one scene)

Exteriors
A Pennine valley (two scenes)
A fairground (one scene)
Outside the prison (two scenes)
A park (one scene)
The Thames Embankment (one scene)
East End streets (two scenes)

A possible place for an interval in stage performance has been suggested in the playscript.

Devising your own documentary
A documentary play (like *Annie Kenney*) can draw on a variety of source material, such as maps, ballads, music, local history collections, *Jackdaws*, letters, diaries, libraries, local government records, church archives, local newspaper files, biographies, specially gathered memories and opinions (e.g. of local old people), etc.

The presentation of a staged documentary might involve drama, both scripted and improvised, slides, tapes, creative lighting, costume, dance, song, live music, sound effects, recorded music, mime, debate, narrative, etc. Possible topics on which documentary plays might be devised include:

1   Historical events (national or local); biographies (of local heroes and heroines such as Annie Kenney); anniversaries.
2   Environmental problems, both local and national.
3   Social problems (strikes, baby-snatching, etc.)
4   Domestic and school issues (pocket money, liberty, effects of TV, etc.)
5   Broader topics such as loneliness, violence, love, the family, holidays, etc.

Acknowledgements

For permission to publish the plays in this volume, the editors are grateful to the following authors and their agents: C.P. Taylor and Dr Jan van Loewen Ltd for Some Enchanted Evening; Tom Hadaway and Iron Magazine for The Filleting Machine; Alan Plater and Margaret Ramsay Ltd for Annie Kenney; Barrie Keeffe and Harvey Unna & Stephen Durbridge Ltd for Here Comes the Sun.

Some Enchanted Evening

C. P. Taylor

Characters

Peter, in his twenties; he lives with his parents on Tyneside and
works in Wills cigarette factory as a packer
A Lass, whom Peter meets in a Newcastle-upon-Tyne social club
Sue, Peter's girlfriend

Dad ⎫ Peter's parents   **Policeman**
Mam ⎭   **Samaritan** (woman)
Character on the bridge   **TV Man**
Woman on the bridge   **Trainer in gymnasium**
Master of Ceremonies and **Bingo Caller** in club

First performed by the Live Theatre, Newcastle, in February 1977
with the following cast:

Peter	David Whittaker
Sue	Anne Orwin
Mam	Pauline Moriarty
Dad	Colin McClaughlin
Girl	Denise Bryson
PE Instructor	
TV Director	Max Roberts
Directed by	Paul Chamberlain
Designer	Phil Bailey
Stage Manager	Brian Hogg

This play is for my wife, Liz, with all my love

Some Enchanted Evening

Scene: **A social club, Newcastle-upon-Tyne. Peter** *is sitting at a table, vodkas and dry gingers in front of him.*

Peter: [*To audience*] I'm sitting at me table in the club, with me vodkas and dry gingers, when this lass comes up. [**Lass** *approaches table*]

Lass: Anybody sitting here?

Peter: Just me. [*To audience*] So she sits down, looking at me vodkas and dry gingers. [*To* **Lass**] Help yourself.

Lass: [*Taking glass*] Ta. . . .

Peter: [*To audience*] Downs her drink like it was lemonade and then says to us. . . .

Lass: You're happy, are you?

Peter: [*To audience*] Now some people might have thought that was a funny kind of remark to make to somebody they'd never seen before in their life. Not me. I know people are off their nut. They're all mad. I mean, look at me. Sitting here, just know. You'd say: That's a normal kind of lad, isn't it? Anyway, I says to her. Explaining why I had a happy look on me face. [*To* **Lass**] Me mam bought us a new table lamp for me bedroom.

Lass: Oh. . . .

Peter: [*To audience*] Then she came out with what you might think was another funny thing.

Lass: *You've* never thought of doin' away with yourself, have you?

Peter: [*To audience*] What do you make of that? Suicide, she meant. [*To* **Lass**] Suicide, you mean?

Lass: [*Studying his face*] Do you always wear your hair that way?

Peter: Got a blow wave. In that place across the road from the central station. Saturday.

Lass: It's nice.

Peter: It is, isn't it? [*To audience*] To tell you the truth, I've got a bit of a problem with me hair . . . I'm not going bald . . . but here and there. . . . Wearing a bit thin. . . .

Lass: Me brother was married this Saturday.

Peter: Same day I had me blow wave.

Lass: Was it?

Peter: [*To audience*] She had a lovely face. That's another thing about us. First thing I look at in a lass is her face.

Lass: Me brother was married on Saturday.

Peter: So you were saying.

Lass: Me lad finished with us on the Thursday, before. . . .

Peter: [*To audience*] And she started crying. [*To* **Lass**. *Pushing over one of his five vodkas and ginger ales*] . . . . Come on, man . . . it's all right. . . . Have another vodka and ginger . . . I've still three left . . . [*To audience*] I always get five, to save us going backwards and forwards to the bar . . . lasts us well to the bingo. . . .

Lass: And I work in Woolco in Killingworth.

Peter: [*To audience*] Don't know what that had to do with anything. . . . Expected us to say something. So I said: [*To*

Lass] I work in Wills, on the Coast Road.

Lass: [*Downing the vodka and ginger ale*] I'm serious, you know. . . .

Peter: That's not lemonade, you know.

Lass: I'm not sure which way to do it . . . I'm frightened in the end, when it comes to the bit, I mightn't be able to. . . . Know what I mean?

Peter: [*To audience*] Now, you'd think that was a funny thing to talk about, first time you chat up a lad, wouldn't you? The best way to do yourself in. But listen to this: [*To* **Lass**] I wouldn't try jumping off the George the Fifth Tyne Bridge. . . . Tell you that!

Lass: No?

Peter: Tried that. . . .

Lass: I never thought about the George the Fifth Bridge. . . . You tried that, did you? [*Reaching out for one of his vodkas and ginger*)

Peter: Better if you sip it slowly . . . get the full flavour. . . . You not see us on Tyne Tees? On 'Look North', too. . . . Came in with the music . . . [*Hums Look North theme*] 'Byker Man in George the Fifth Bridge Drama'.

Lass: Honest. . . .

Peter: Honest. . . . Straight. . . . I did. . . .

Lass: You really did?

Peter: [*To* **Lass**] Yeah. . . .

Lass: That's nice. That's the first good thing that's happened to us for weeks. Did you feel like, there was just nothing to look forward to . . . ever again . . . in your whole life. . . .

Peter: Nothing. . . . Lass finished with us – like your lad.

Lass: Listen. Don't cry, pet.

Peter: [*To audience*] I wasn't crying. But you don't like to disappoint people, do you? [*To* **Lass**] I'll try. . . . See . . . I'm climbing up the girders of the George the Fifth Bridge. [*Standing on chair*] Sunday morning. . . . Very rough they were, them girders. . . . Apart from anything else . . . freezing cold. [*To audience*] Hadn't got my foot on the third girder, when this character starts shouting at us.

Character: Where you going?

Peter: Painting the bridge.

Character: It's a Sunday.

Peter: Overtime.

Character: Oh. [*about to go*] You haven't any paint.

Peter: In me pocket.

Character: Or overalls. Or scaffolding. You're up to something. Come on. Come down!

Peter: Piss off! [*To audience*] Shouldn't have said that. I mean. . . . It's not as if I'm given to bad language, anyway.

Character: You're from the IRA . . . aren't you?

Peter: [*To audience*] Went on climbing.

Character: You are. You're going to blow up the bridge. I can see that . . . I don't understand the mentality of you maniacs! Bringing suffering and destruction to innocent people who —

Peter: [*To audience*] Probably on his way to the Bigg Market to preach to anybody daft enough to listen to him.

Character: Prepared to sacrifice anything for the sake of a boundary line. . . . To further your own destructiveness and wickedness. . . .

Peter: I'm not from the IRA, man. I come from Byker. Union bloody Road!

Character: I'll make a note of that. That's where your bomb factory is, is it? Now, listen to me. Did you know every

British citizen has the right to arrest somebody if he thinks he is behaving in a suspicious manner?

Peter: [*To audience*] I didn't know that, did you?

Character: [*brandishing his umbrella*] I arrest you. Come down immediately.

Peter: Piss off, man, will you! [*To audience*] Says me, climbing a bit higher up. I had to pick a bloody Sunday. Millions of people all over the place down at the quayside. . . . By that time, other characters had turned up. Somebody saw a copper down at the quayside and started shouting for him.

Somebody: [*Shouting*] Police! Police! [*Waving*]

Woman: Never there when they're needed. Could blow up the whole of Newcastle, while they're sitting in their little boxes, drinking their tea and digestives.

Peter: [*To audience*] I was having a rough time, all round. Them girders were freezing. And it was cold. One of these east winds coming from the sea. I should've put me heavy coat on. . . . But I'm the same size as me Dad and he might as well get some good out of it . . . I thought.

All: [*Shouting*] Police! Police!

Peter: [*To audience*] They were all so busy shouting down at the quayside for a copper, they didn't see this big policeman coming from the Gateshead side. I like Gateshead people. I have a lot of time for them.

Policeman: Just make room will you? Thank you . . . Thank you . . . . Get back, now . . . please. . . . Thank you. . . .

Peter: I'm not an IRA man, sir.

Character: I've got the address of his bomb factory, officer. Union Road.

Peter: [*To* **Policeman**] That's where I *live*, man!

Policeman: I've got a bad back, sir. Would you mind coming down and sparing us having to crick me neck, having to talk up to you, there. . . .

Peter: I've nothing to do with the IRA. All I'm doing is jumping off the bridge.

Policeman: I'm afraid not, sir.

Peter: I am.

Policeman: You know, of course, that's illegal, sir.

Peter: Not going to worry me, that, is it? At the bottom of the Tyne down there.

Policeman: Would you like to give me some particulars, sir? Just . . . in the event of an accident happening. . . . Next of kin . . . address and so on. . . . Saves us a lot of trouble. Haven't to go all over the place chasing your identity . . . waiting till they drag you up from the bottom, sir. . . .

Peter: [*To audience*] See what I mean about Gateshead chaps. Pulled out his transistor and started chatting away to it.

Policeman: Just getting the Police boat. . . . Might be a bit before it turns up. Somebody's thrown a dead donkey into the river down at Howdon.

Peter: Nothing to do with me. I'm definitely doing myself in.

Policeman: Off the record, if you want to talk about it. I can't stop you. It's my duty to listen to you and try to persuade you not to jump. At the same time . . . I've got a terrible back, so. . . . Been in the RVI for it and everything . . . lying on a board . . . tried acupuncture . . . ever tried acupuncture?

Peter: No.

Policeman: Should try it. Maybe done better for you than me. Even went to this woman in Rothbury. . . . Mends backs . . . called the witch of Rothbury. . . . You ever heard of her?

Peter: [*To audience*] I was looking down at the quayside. All the crowds had twigged to what was happening. Looking up at us. . . . Everything down there had come to a dead stop. Even the

Paki who sells tea towels and sheets had given up his patter to watch what was happening. . . .

Policeman: That's why I'm the wrong kind of a chap to be talking to would-be suicides. This back of mine . . . the way I am. Keeps making us see the black side of life. See what I mean? Getting us down. Even spoiling me bit of fun with the lass, now and then.

Peter: [*To audience*] When I looked on at the river. Pitch black. Bits of rubbish floating all over the place. Bloody poisonous, the minute I hit it. . . . Worst thing was it looked cold. . . . I hate being cold! And this bloody copper kept on about his rotten back.

Policeman: If it carries on like this. Tell you straight, son. Going to finish us for promotion . . . and the pound going to hell. Millions of unemployed. Violence and vandalism, all over the world. Can't even walk round Presto's for a packet of Daz, without having to keep your eye open, some daft bugger hasn't planted a bomb for Ireland or Palestine or Pakistan or bloody Chungking!

Peter: [*To audience*] Right raver I'd got here! Just getting on to the way everybody was dying from heart diseases from eating too much butter when this lass turns up, in a yellow Mini. . . . Could see she was somebody official. . . .

Policeman: Move on, please, miss. Thank you.

Samaritan: Samaritans. Message was passed on from Pilgrim Street Police Station.

Policeman: Oh. Samaritans.

Samaritan: [*To* **Peter**] Hullo. I've brought you a flask of tea. Like some tea?

Peter: I'm going to jump. I mean . . . I don't want to waste your time.

Samaritan: Let's talk about it, for a while, can we?

Policeman: [*watching her organizing the flask on a rope*] I only hope you know what you're doing, miss. . . . I said they should send a minister. . . .

Samaritan: I think he's coming, too.

Peter: [*To audience*] Bloody dying for a cup of tea.

Samaritan: You look terribly cold.

Peter: I'm all right.

Samaritan: Look . . . would you like a biscuit or something. That was stupid of me. I should've thought of that.

Peter: [*To audience*] Could've done with a Kit Kat . . . just fancied one. [*To her*] Wouldn't mind a Kit Kat.

Samaritan: Officer . . . I wonder if you'd mind nipping down to the quayside and bringing up a Kit Kat. . . .

Policeman: And leave him, up there. . . .

Samaritan: Just for a mintue. He'll be all right till you come back.

Policeman: [*Taking money*] A Kit Kat?

Peter: Or a Mars Bar, if you can't get a Kit Kat.

Policeman: Should be able to get a Kit Kat. Newcastle'll be coming to something right enough if I can't get you a Kit Kat on the quayside on a Sunday morning. [*Going*] You all right, up there, then?

Samaritan: [*Watching **Peter** drinking*] I didn't sugar it too much?

Peter: It's all right. Not bad. [*To audience*] With the copper away, people had started to come up to see what was happening. Couldn't blame them. . . . Bit of a change from the usual patter down at the quayside. . . . Started talking to her. Suppose what you call 'open my heart out'. [*To **Samaritan***] See, Sue works for Securicor. [*To audience*] Lass that I was engaged to and that caused all the trouble. Don't get us wrong.

Not one of those big heavies with a truncheon swinging from their belt ... and a helmet. I mean she had a *helmet*. Drives a van with documents. Not money. ...

Samaritan: You work for Securicor, too, do you?

Peter: [*To audience*] That was the trouble. I don't. [*To* **Samaritan**] I work for Wills ... on the Coast Road. [*To audience*] I was going to me work. She was coming out, delivering documents. [**Sue** *comes out*] [*To audience*] *She* saw *me* first.

Sue: Did I see you last Saturday at the Killingworth Carnival?

Peter: [*To audience*] That was a new one on us! Killingworth Carnival! [*To* **Sue**] *Me?*

Sue: My mam's on the Benwell Lancers' committee.

Peter: [*To audience*] I wasn't very quick on the uptake, them days. ... [*To* **Sue**] Is she?

Sue: You work in Wills, do you?

Peter: Yeah. [*To audience*] I mean what the hell would I be doing there?

Sue: You like it?

Peter: Cannie. ... [*To audience*] It was ... smashing job. ... I mean ... had its ups and downs like all jobs. Specially after I took up with Sue. But that'll come out later.

Sue: Wasn't you, then, was it? At Killingworth.

Peter: No.

Sue: Somebody spitting image. Same nice brown hair. ...

Peter: [*To audience*] See what I mean? Nobody's ever said anything about me hair before.

Sue: And eyes ... big eyes like yours. ...

Peter: [*To audience*] Be honest with you. Whole trouble from the beginning was I've led what you call a sheltered life. You can see, from me mam and dad. ... [**Mam** *and* **Dad** *enter*]

They're not what you'd call raving it up together. I mean . . .
only thing me dad used me mam for was a cheap hot water
bottle in winter. [*To audience*] Back to outside Wills.

Sue: I'm not keeping you from your work?

Peter: No . . . I'm a bit early.

Sue: Early bird, gets the worm.

Peter: [*To audience*] Thing is. To be honest with you. I
couldn't believe any lass would fancy us. I mean . . . look at
us. . . . Be honest, I'm nothing to look at, am I? So . . . when
this lass fancies us . . . and even *I* got that message! . . . I mean
. . . *her*. Fancying *me*. . . . Look at her.

Sue: [*taking helmet off*] Bit hot these.

Peter: Yeah. [*To audience*] Stood there a minute . . . not
speaking. . . . Then she says . . .

Sue: Better get going. See you . . . ?

Peter: Yeah. . . .

Sue: [*turning back*] Oh. Do you mind us asking? You're not
going steady or anything, are you . . . ?

Peter: No.

Sue: Neither am I.

Peter: Good.

Sue: Is it?

Peter: I mean. . . .

Sue: [*Going again. It's hopeless*] See you.

Peter: Yeah.

Sue: [*Turning back. Last try*] Do you like the pictures?

Peter: Yeah.

Sue: Fancy going, tonight. . . . I mean. . . . If you're not
doing anything.

Peter: I'm not. . . . [*To audience*] So that was us fixed up.

We went to see 'One Flew Over the Cuckoo's Nest'. I paid the pictures. She bought the sweets and ice-cream. Bought us half a pound of Quality Street. To be honest with you, I ate most of them, meself. . . . Had to say excuse us, every time I wanted one. So she let go of me hand. [*As he is talking the* **Policeman** *comes back*]

Policeman: No question about it . . . something is seriously wrong with this country. . . . Not a Kit Kat on the whole quayside. . . . Got you a couple of Penguins . . . all right?

Peter: I don't mind Penguins.

Policeman: How's he doing, then? Coming down, yet, son?

Peter: Have a bite to eat, then I'll jump.

Policeman: Come on. . . . [*To crowds*] Move back there. They're fetching your mother and father. . . . Sent a car for them.

Peter: Man, you shouldn't have done that.

Policeman: Having a job getting a minister. But they've a rabbi coming from Gateshead. Bad time, Sunday mornings for ministers. But all right for Rabbis. . . . The Jews' Sunday's on a Saturday. Did you know that?

Peter: Sunday on a Saturday?

Policeman: Whole place is alive with rabbis, Gateshead. . . . Tripping over them wherever you go.

Peter: It was lovely, the first couple of months together . . . Me and Sue. . . . You know what I mean. . . . Like in outer space. [**Lass** *is sniffing at him. To audience*] Middle of me telling her all this . . . she starts sniffing at us. I mean . . . you don't like people sniffing at you. . . . I definitely had me deodorant on. . . . Use it twice a day . . . after brushing me teeth in the morning and shaving at night.

Lass: Trying to recognize your after-shave. . . .

Peter: Oh. . . .

Lass: I like a man to use a nice after-shave. . . .

Peter: Yeah . . . so do I. . . . I mean . . . you know what I mean. . . .

Lass: Not Old Spice. . . .

Peter: Denim. Me mam bought us it last Xmas. . . .

Lass: That's it, Denim. Lovely.

Peter: Is it?

Lass: He used Hai Karate. We used to do that advert. You know? . . . He'd come into the room . . . with his Hair Karate . . . and I'd pounce on him. . . .

Peter: [*backing away*] Did you?

Lass: But I like Denim, better . . . I think. . . . It suits you. . . .

Peter: You reckon? Don't know what it is about us that excites women. Exactly the same thing with Sue. At times, she got really excited. . . . Know what I mean. I got this book in the Covered-in-Market . . . *Married Bliss* . . . that told you exactly what to do. But I didn't want to rush things. That's the trouble with the liberation of lasses, isn't it? They rush you. It's all right for them. The fella's got to do all the work, hasn't he? I'm not saying I don't enjoy it. But I like to take my time about these things. I know nobody bothers about principles nowadays. But I'd rather save it till we'd been to the church, and she has a ring on her finger.

Sue: [*Cuddling him*] That's all right, pet. Just take your time. I love you . . . I just thought . . . if you were getting too frustrated. . . .

Peter: No . . . I'm all right.

Sue: [*kissing him*] Good. Do you love us?

Peter: Course I love you. [*To audience*] I did. Bloody mad about her. . . . Thought about her all my waking time. In

Wills . . . out of Wills . . . in bed. . . . Wake up during the night, thinking about her . . . I mean . . . it was really something, wasn't it. I had a lass at last of me own. . . . Me dad was a bit disappointed. Minute I told her, me mam said I had to bring her straight up to the house. Me dad started on one of these speeches of his about the Breeding Force. Never know *what he's* on about when he starts going; like that. . . .

Dad: What I'm saying is . . . you're up against a force out of yer control . . . The Breeding Force.

Mam: I'm talking about when the lass comes, man. Do us a favour and don't come out with that old story of yours, the night a bomb hit yer crane.

Dad: Don't know what I'm bothering for, son. *Speaking* to you, people don't listen to people, anyway. Do they? Especially yer own kids.

Peter: [*To audience*] See what I mean?

Dad: But I am speaking as a man, who has had very limited experience of the opposite sex. Time Sodom and Gomorrah came to Byker, it was a bit late in the day for us. [**Peter** *staring blank at him. What's he on about, now?*] I'm talking about the Permissiveness, man. Everybody throwing the Ten Commandments on the rubbish heap. . . .

Mam: Could you not put a *tie* on, for God's sake.

Dad: Nobody wears ties, now, man. I mean . . . its up to you. But I wouldn't advise you to get stuck like I did. I mean . . . it was understandable in my situation. I didn't know anything about anything till me wedding night.

Mam: And then ye were too drunk to do anything about it.

Dad: I mean. You've a situation nowadays where they're doing it on the bloody *streets*, aren't they. . . .

Mam: Jimmie, man. . . .

Dad: He reads the *News of the World* same as you and me. . . .

What I'm saying is . . . watch it . . . be careful . . . see what I mean. It's a force beyond yer control. . . . I know. . . . See what I'm getting at, son? You realize the *consequences* of yer *actions*. Do you, son?

Mam: If he doesn't, it's a bit late in the day telling him, now, isn't it?

Dad: Is it? Has he?

Mam: I'm not talking about that, man. Of course he hasn't. . . . Have you, Peter . . . ? Not my lad. . . .

Dad: All I am saying is, son.

Mam: Go and brush yer teeth. Ye can smell the curry from them chop suey rolls ye had for yer tea, minute ye come through the door.

Dad: Fair enough. Ye've got yerself a lass at long last. But I would not advise ye te follow in yer father's footsteps. Do not make yer first yer last.

Mam: What do ye mean by that, like? You didn't take any hurt by it, did you?

Dad: If I did, bugger all I can do about it now. All I'm saying to the lad is: Make sure you don't have any accidents that's going to get ye tied up in knots before ye know it. One Minute at Te Kerb. Right? Take precautions. That's all I'm saying to you, son . . . I know. . . . I'm bloody wasting my breath. Same time. . . .

Mam: Jimmie, man! Ye're giving the lad ideas.

Peter: No, he's not, mam.

Mam: [*Worried*] Is he not, son?

Peter: [*To audience*] We went to Jesmond Dene, most of the time. . . . Odd times, Heaton Park. . . . Lot of times to Pet's Corner . . . spent hours in Pet's Corner, looking at the guinea pigs and rabbits. . . .

Sue: I'd like our children to have a nice pet, when they're old enough, wouldn't you?

Peter: [*To audience*] Not even *engaged* yet! [*To* **Sue**] Yeah. . . .

Sue: Fancy one of these houses, overlooking the Dene. Green all round you. Do you?

Peter: Yeah. [*To audience*] I did . . . I *think*.

Samaritan: It's always a nice time. The first few months, getting to know one another. Isn't it . . . ?

Peter: Like that song. 'Getting To Know You'. . . . *Rose Marie*?

Policeman: That's it . . . from *Rose Marie*.

[On the stage the band has struck up 'Getting To Know You']

MC: The Singing Policeman . . . going to give you the 'Drinking Song' from the Student Prince . . . [**Singer** *launches into* Getting To Know You. **MC** *shrugs his shoulders. After the song, the band playing very softly under dialogue,* Getting to Know You]

Peter: [*To audience*] We went to the Pet's Cemetery, too, in The Dene. That's where she asked us to get engaged.

Sue: Do you think we should get engaged, now, Peter?

Peter: Would *you* bury your Tibbie here, if she died?

Sue: She deserves it, doesn't she? What about getting engaged, then?

Peter: Engaged . . . I'd like to bury our Ginger here. . . . You mean. Engaged. I mean. What do you mean like. Sue. Engaged. You know what I mean. [*To audience*] You know what I mean.

Sue: You've enough money for a nice ring. Doesn't need to be expensive. There's nearly £780 in your PO savings.

Peter: [*To audience*] I never kept anything back from her. . . .

She liked to know these things. How much I had in me savings. [*To* **Sue**] I'd have to ask me mam and dad.

Sue: What's it got to do with them, Peter, man?

Peter: It's a big responsibility, isn't it? Getting engaged. . . .

Sue: Peter, pet. Your mam and dad aren't going to live for ever, love.

Peter: I know. . . .

Sue: You love us, don't you?

Peter: I do, man. [*To audience*] I did.

Sue: I'm thinking of asking the doctor to put us on the Pill.

Peter: What's the matter, Sue? Are you bad?

Sue: Peter, you know what I'm talking about. The Pill.

Peter: Oh. The Pill. . . .

Sue: I mean. Now we're engaged.

Lass: I'm not sure about the Pill. . . .

Peter: No.

Lass: It does things to your body . . . I'm not talking about thrombosis. . . . Your breasts. . . . And some people it affects their passion.

Peter: Does it?

Lass: He was all for us going on the Pill. . . . Was your lass on it?

Peter: [*To audience*] Just told her, didn't I? [*To* **Sue**] I told you.

Lass: I said to him . . . in the meantime, you can take charge of the precautions. . . . Later on . . . I might go to one of them clinics. . . . But I'm definitely not going to start messing about with my bodily functions. . . . Mind, I made damn sure he *did* take precautions. Good job, too, isn't it. The way things turned out. Do you like kids?

Peter: Kids?

Lass: You know. Having kids.

Peter: I haven't had any yet. . . .

Lass: I like kids. . . .

Peter: So do I. . . .

Lass: That's nice. . . . That's a good basis for a couple to start on, isn't it? . . . He didn't like kids. . . . He used to say, what's great about having kids. . . . I said, you'll think differently when you're married. . . . That's what you think, he said. . . . Ruins yer love life, kids . . . that's what he always said. . . . How many kids would you like?

Peter: Kids?

Lass: I'd just want about four in the end. . . . No more. . . . That's enough, isn't it?

Peter: Oh, yeah. . . . Definitely. . . .

Lass: I mean. I'm talking if I decided to go on. . . .

Peter: Go on. . . .

Lass: *Living*. Not doing myself in.

Peter: Oh. [*To audience*] Anyway. . . . It was easy enough for her. All she had to do was tell us we were engaged and that was it. *I* had to tell me mam and dad. . . . And before I got round to it, she'd got us to buy her a ring for £37.69 in Northern Goldsmiths. . . . Had to tell them sharp, then, before Sue got on to them. . . . Me dad started going on about colour telly's rotting me brain, minute I asked him.

Dad: All the things people need to live, them days. . . . Colour tellies. Cars. Tape recorders. Transistors. Go into a house nowadays and it's like bloody Space Control in Dallas Houston, ready to blast off.

Mam: We're trying to find out whose idea it was, man. For them to get engaged. It wasn't *yours*, was it, now Peter?

Dad: All this bloody money we're lending from the Germans and Yanks and Japs. To buy all that bloody rubbish. . . . No wonder we're in debt up to the eyes. What bloody for?

Mam: Now, listen to me, son. Sue is the first lass you ever went out with.

Dad: What do people need to live, for God's sake? Eh? A bed . . . suit, a fire and roof over yer head. . . . Pound of sausages.

Mam: I want to hear what Peter has to say for himself, man. Will ye shut yer gob a minute? Listen, son. I can see exactly what's happening. She's got you where you don't know where you are.

Dad: Half a dozen eggs. Sacks of potatoes. Odd pint now and then. Who bloody needs a colour television. Rots yer brain, that's all that does.

Mam: And who bloody sits in front of it all night, like their bum was nailed to the chair. . . .

Dad: I'm telling you, amn't I? It's like a drug. . . . They've got me hypnotized like everybody else.

Mam: I'll be honest with you. This is yer first romance, son. You can't see clearly, what's happening to you.

Dad: And that bloody car . . . out there! Who needs bloody cars. . . . If everybody got shot of their cars . . . I mean. . . . How long can we go on like this? Everybody locked up in their houses in front of the telly or their bloody cars. . . . Don't even talk to a strange face when they go to Whitley Bay at the weekends. . . . You remember the excitement, going down to the central station for the electric train to the coast. . . .

Mam: We're talking about Peter's engagement, man.

Dad: I'm not in the mood to get involved with his stupid bloody problems. Just now, man. I've had twenty-six years of him. Let somebody else worry about him, now.

Mam: Who bloody started in the first place, getting on to the boy, about not making his first his last.

Dad: Talking about *me* wasn't I? If I was in the same position as he is today, I wouldn't make the same mistake twice. But he's not me. And thank God, I'm not him. I don't see any reason why just because I fathered you, son, I have to think the sun shines out of yer behind.

Mam: Will ye let the lad speak, man. This is one of the most important decisions he has to make in his life. And when he comes to us for a bit of advice, all ye can talk about is about bloody colour tellies and trains to the coast. Now ... Peter, pet. Do you want te know what yer mam thinks?

Peter: Yes ... mam. But I—

Mam: Right, then.

Peter: I know, mam, Sue's—

Mam: I'll be honest with you, Peter. She's a cannie enough lass in her own way.

Dad: Anyway, I wouldn't give it more than eleven or twelve years. and it'll all bloody blow up.

Mam: Will you let the lad speak, man, for God's sake!

Peter: You see, mam ... I know. . . .

Mam: I'll tell you what we'll do, Peter.

Dad: They'll either drop a bomb on us ... or bloody Windscale'll blow us all up. . . . By that time, I'll be six feet under, and well out the bugger, anyway. . . . It's *your* problem, son.

Mam: What we'll do, son ... is wait a year or so. Till ye know yer own mind a bit better. That's the best thing. Yes. That's what yer father and I have decided. Haven't we, Jimmie?

Dad: I'm not interested, man. . . . In him getting engaged. Or not engaged. I've bigger problems in me mind, just now. . . . If ye are thinking of getting engaged, son, I'll just say this te ye. Engagements rings cost *money*. Wouldn't get an engagement ring them days under twenty quid. Is it worth it? Ask yerself, son [*Looking at* **Mam**] Is it *bloody* worth it?

Mam: So that's settled, then. We'll just wait on a bit till ye know yer own mind a bit better, Peter, pet.

Peter: [*To audience*] Me luck was in but. Sometimes it is, isn't it? Same day, Mrs Cartwright, two doors down, bumped into me mam and told her her lass had got engaged and asked her and me dad in for a drink.

Mam: [*To* **Dad**] I was thinking over about the lad getting engaged, Jimmie.

Dad: See if it was up to us, we'd have another Battle of Britain. That's the difference between my generation and yours, son. . . . All you can think about is yer own pleasure. . . .

Peter: [*To audience*] Me dad was reading the *Chronicle* front page about tabs and beer going up again and the pound going down.

Mam: If the boy's heart's set on it.

Peter: It is, mam.

Dad: Not that I'm saying there's anything wrong with pleasure. . . . But how long can ye go on with a nation of playboys like your generation, son?

Mam: And you really think she's Miss Right?

Peter: I do, mam.

Mam: It's only an *engagement,* Jimmie. It's not getting married. You don't need to get a divorce if an engagement doesn't work out.

Dad: See what we'd've done, son, was battleships all round the coast line. Bombers and fighters . . . repelling anybody trying to get here with their cheap-jack washing machines and cars. . . . See what I mean . . . I mean . . . for Christ's sake. . . . We can make bloody cars here, can't we? . . . Where's the sense in shipping them right across the world from Japan and bloody Hong Kong. . . .

Mam: We're talking about the engagement, man. The boy wants to get engaged.

Dad: So long as he doesn't expect any expensive presents. The state the pound's in just now, I'd think twice about buying meself a pint of Federation!

Peter: Week after we got engaged, Sue started working on us.

Policeman: Wait on. . . . Squad car. . . . [*Sound of car*]

Samaritan: Is that your mother and father, Peter?

Peter: Could do without bloody them, just now!

Mam: [*Going up to the* **Policeman**] I want to report these two, for dragging us here. Bringing us out on a Sunday morning. . . . I told them straight, it's not my lad. You've got the wrong Peter Simmonds. . . . Sundays. Peter goes out to North Shields Pier, fishing. I want to speak to somebody in authority about this. Frightening decent people. Sending policemen in uniform to their houses. God knows what people'll think we've been up to. . . . Me lad's going to jump off the George The Fifth– [*Sees* **Peter**, *at last*] Peter! Peter! Get down from there! This instant! Will you bloody get down from there! I'm warning you!

Peter: [*To audience*] Started to drizzle on top of everything else. And her down there. . . . With her red face. Screaming at us.

Mam: Get down! Get bloody down!

Peter: [*To audience*] Thought, Christ! Go back to Byker and spend the rest of my days with these two!

Mam: [*To* **Dad**] Are you not going to do something for God's sake! Will you get that boy down, man!

Policeman: It's all right, madam. We're trying to get a ladder.

Mam: Peter! Peter! Get down from there! Do you hear me?

[*To audience*] Will you bloody say something to him, man!

Dad: [*Looking up*] Nothing compared to the height of some of the cranes I've worked on.

Mam: The boy's going to jump into the river.

Dad: What can I bloody do about it, man!

Policeman: Just calm yerself. Missus . . . just got a message over me radio. Rabbi coming any minute. Now.

Mam: Look at him up there! How can I calm down. Peter. . . . Be careful . . . you'll fall off. My God. What have I done to deserve this!

Policeman: You want a Penguin? Bought one for me break. But you're welcome to have it.

Dad: See. . . it's a key job . . . working a crane down the yard.

Policeman: Sure it is.

Mam: Will you say something to him, man.

Dad: What can I say to him, woman! [*To* **Peter**, *embarrassed*] Hullo, Peter. . . .

Peter: Hullo, Dad.

Mam: Is that all you can say?

Dad: I'm telling the policeman here about me crane, man, amn't I? . . . What's the use of talking to him. . . . [*To* **Policeman**] It's not their fault. It's just the world they've grown up in . . . messed up the whole generation.

Policeman: He'll be all right. He's young . . . and he's got a good back.

Mam: [*Shouting*] Peter, will you bloody come down from there! Come down! [*As she is screaming the* **TV Man** *arrives with his camera*]

TV Man: Excuse me.

Mam: Bloody come down this instant, you rotten swine!

If you don't bloody come down I'll— [*Sees* **TV Man**. *Breaks off*] Eee. We're not on telly, are we?

TV Man: Mr and Mrs Simmonds?

Mam: That's me. He's Mr Simmonds. Eee . . . I rushed out the house. You'll have te excuse me appearance. As soon as the police knocked at the door. I just put on the first thing I could lay me hands on. I'd take off me scarf, but I hadn't even time to put a comb through me hair.

TV Man: Understand the situation, Mrs Simmonds. Let me assure you of this. This is going to be *positive* television. I am only interested in the bright side of life. . . . [*To* **Peter**] I know exactly how you feel, Peter. That's the only message that seems to come out in the papers and my own television medium. What a terrible world we're living in. Not a ray of hope wherever you turn. Now let me say this. I am convinced that this is one of the best times in the history of people.

Policeman: Is it?

Peter: [*To audience*] Another bloody nut.

Dad: [*Pushing himself forward*] I'm the lad's father. I'm just telling the officer here about me crane.

TV Man: Great. Fair enough. There are a few kids kicking each other's heads in from time to time. Few idiots in Ireland blowing each other up.

Dad: See. It's a key position. On the cranes. The heart of the shipyards.

TV Man: It must be. What I'm saying is. Look at 1914-18. 1939. *Tens* of millions killed. Millions every week. . . . Compared to then, this is paradise, today. It's a new world, isn't it?

Dad: That's what I'm talking about. The war. To give you an idea how important the job is. During the war. Even Hitler knew me name.

TV Man: Exactly. [*To* **Peter**] Hitler is dead, now. Think of that, before you jump.

Mam: Do you think he's going to jump?

Dad: Mebbe's not exactly *Hitler*. But Lord Haw-Haw knew us.

Peter: [*To audience*] On to his one story again. Him and Lord Haw-Haw.

Dad: On that night . . . 1943. . . . In Walker Naval Yard. . . .

TV Man: All this talk about Britain being finished, now. . . . Have you ever been on the Town Moor on a windy Sunday afternoon?

Mam: He was always a good, sensible level-headed boy. A lovely, thoughtful, dutiful son. . . . Steady job in Wills. . . . I don't know what's come over him.

Dad: I'm telling him about me crane, man.

TV Man: Kites. All over the place. On the Town Moor. You can guide them by hand. First man-controlled kites in history. . . . Who invented them? A Britisher. . . .

Dad: That's what I say. The Dunkirk spirit. That's what's needed today. Now . . . I was in me cabin. . . . Direct hit on me crane.

TV Man: Do you know we've sold ten million kites to Japan, alone. British ingenuity, Peter. All right. So the pound's having its ups and downs, just now. But the whole county's floating on a sea of oil.

Mam: What it is, is just a bit of trouble with his lass. You know what the lasses are like, these days. Out for owt they can get.

Dad: I was in me cabin. I was in me cabin. Direct hit on me crane. And that same night. Ask anybody, and they'll tell you. *I* didn't hear it, meself . . . I'd better things te do than listen to bloody traitors to their country on the wireless. But on that night. Lord Haw-Haw. That was William Joyce. You've heard of Lord Haw-Haw.

TV Man: Yes. The world is a beautiful place, even on the waste grounds down there. Flowers are growing.

Dad: Broadcast a message: 'Are you there, Jimmie Simmonds? Keep off your crane, tonight, Bonnie lad. You're going to have an unexpected visitor.' That was the message. . . . Ask anybody. . . .

Policeman: That a fact?

Dad: Ask anybody . . . Lord Haw-Haw knew me name. That'll show you how vital I was to the war effort. What I'm saying is where would we have been today, if our generation had been as soft and flabby and spineless as his lot there. Eh? . . . Bloody swastika flying over Buckingham Palace, if it'd been up to that lot. . . . Rotten Krauts ruling the world. . . .

Policeman: Nearly doing it, just now, aren't they?

Dad: You're right. Got a point there.

TV Man: Skylarks are singing on the Town Moor. A few miles down in the river, Peter, children are playing by the sea. The world is a beautiful place.

Policeman: Like that song. 'The Hills are Alive with Music' from the *Jungle Book*.

[*He sings the song. Sound of music.* **Peter** *gestures*]

TV Man: I think he wants to say something. Hold the mike up.

Peter: Did you say you had another Penguin?

Policeman: Just given it to your Dad . . . he's eating it.

Peter: [*To audience*] Bloody would!

[**Bingo Seller** *approaches their table*]

Sue: Fancy a card?

Peter: Yeah. Might be our lucky night [*To* **Seller**] Give us four.

Sue: I'll pay for mine.

Peter: No, man. I'm loaded [*To audience*] Tell you what happened after the Bingo.

[*Bingo session starts*]

Act 2

Scene: **The social club.** *The bingo session is over.*

Peter: I was sweating there . . . see us?

Lass: Loosen your shirt.

Peter: No. I mean, waiting for a doctor's orders.

Lass: I'll tell you something. I think you've got a nice body. I don't go for these hard, bony men. I like something you can really cuddle.

Peter: Do you?

Lass: And not too many hairs on his chest. Just . . . enough, to show the difference. Do you have many? Let's see.

Peter: No. People are looking. [*To audience*] Vodkas and ginger were definitely going to her head.

Lass: Don't be a spoilsport . . . show us. [*Looks at his shirt*]

Peter: People are looking at us, man.

Lass: Are you shy? I missed that in *him*. I like a bit of shyness. Did you take your clothes off in the dark with her? When I come to think of it . . . that upset us a bit about him. He always had to have the light on. And I didn't like some of the underpants he wore. Different colours. What kind do you wear?

Peter: Wear what?

Lass: I like plain white in a man. Do you not? You don't go in for that last fancy underwear like women's, do you?

Peter: Just what me mam buys us. . . . Never bother.

Lass: [*Looking at him*] Yeah. Just right your body. Don't let anybody tell you it isn't. Mine's not bad, either. Is it? I mean . . . I've been crying a bit and my face isn't looking its best. . . .

Peter: No. It's very nice. It is. . . .

Lass: Is it?

Peter: It is.

Lass: That's another thing. *He* never said anything about my face. *His* mind was on other things.

Peter: Telling you about that sports do. . . . She made us run in.

Lass: Did she make you run?

Peter: Telling you. [*To audience*] See what it is. I'm not one of these characters that worries about their body. That's not my scene. Like a nice night in front of the telly with a bottle of cider and a half pound of Quality Street. Pictures. Going out for a curry. But Sue. First week we were engaged, she took us to this sports do for the Benwell Lancers. Pushed us into going in for the 100 yards open. [*To Sue, taking off his jacket for the race*] I can't run, Sue, man. You know that.

Sue: Come on. Me mam's watching us. Get into the starting line.

Peter: [*To audience*] Bloody *was* watching us, too. Her mam. Sitting up there with the other committee. Only she was wearing this uniform with a helmet. Bits of gold all over. Must have a thing in that family. Helmets and uniforms. Pushed us to the starting line. Had to walk the last twenty yards. [*To Sue*] Told you, I couldn't run.

Sue: It's what's been worrying us for a long time, pet. You're not really fit. Some of the men in Securicor, love. You should see the bodies they have on them.

Peter: I know, Sue. I'm nothing to look at.

Sue: You are. You're just letting yourself go. All these chocolate biscuits and Quality Street.

Peter: [*To audience*] *She* started us on the Quality Street!

Sue: And fish suppers. *Double* fish suppers. Sitting in front of the telly all night. And standing at the machine all day in Wills. . . . Chain-smoking from the start to the end of the shift.

Peter: Get them for free, Sue, man. Doesn't cost us anything.

Sue: Just costs you your lungs and your body. That's all. . . . I mean. I'm not nagging you, love . . . I'd hate that. To be a nagging wife like your mam. If I ever start to nag at you, you tell me. Will you, pet?

Peter: Yeah. . . .

Sue: It's just you could really have a great body, pet. . . . If you just looked after it a bit. Tell you what. One of the lads on the bread vans. He goes to training session three times a week. At the sports centre in Wallsend. Should see his muscles.

Peter: [*To audience*] Yeah. I mean. He needs them, doesn't he. Hunking around big trays of bread all over the place. [*To* **Sue**] Wallsend.

Sue: Just try it for a few nights. See how you get on. It just gets us, pet. When I know how you really could develop yourself. And we just sit night after night in front of the telly.

Peter: Go to the pictures, twice a week, don't we?

Sue: I'll ask him to take you along. Will I, love?

Peter: I don't like missing a night seeing you, Sue. [*To audience*] I didn't. . . .

Sue: You'll be *doing* it for *me*, won't you?

[**Peter** *at a training session*]

Trainer: Come on there! On your feet, Simmonds!

Peter: [*To audience*] Talk about the bloody Nazis! . . . Himmler is alive and well and living in Wallsend Sports Centre.

Trainer: [*Throwing him medicine ball*] Quick! [**Peter** *knocked flat on his back with the weight*] That's the stuff!

Peter: Bit too heavy for me. Not got a lighter ball?

Trainer: Medicine ball, isn't it? . . . On your toes. . . . Look at that belly on you. Look like a tart up the spout!

Peter: [*To audience*] Wasn't all that bad, was I?

Trainer: I'm giving you two weeks, Simmonds. Right? If that belly's not as flat as that football pitch there. You're for it. . . . Right?

Peter: Yeah . . . right. . . .

Trainer: Bit of skipping . . . right? Get all that tobacco poison out of you. You're inhaling all day in that poison factory.

Peter: [*To audience*] Don't know what they all had against Wills. . . . Everybody getting on to us about it. . . . Jealous, that was all. Me getting free tabs all day.

Trainer: Skip, man! For pets' sake! You never learned to skip! Forget it! Ten laps at the double round the track. Right!

Peter: Right! Heil Hitler!

Trainer: [*Calling him back*] Simmonds!

Peter: Yeah. . . .

Trainer: [*Grabbing him*] I took you on here, only because Jackie went down on his knees and said you were his mate and ready to sweat blood to get fit. . . . You listen to me. . . . You respond to discipline here, or piss off back to your drug factory.

Peter: It's not a bloody drug factory! It's a cigarette factory. . . . You know it's a cigarette factory.

Trainer: That's all I'm saying to you. You've been warned.

Peter: Gives a bit of happiness to millions of people. That factory. Doesn't it? Everybody moaning about rotten lung cancer.

Trainer: *Simmonds!*

Peter: *Do* you? Bet you know plenty people knocked down by cars and lorries?

Trainer: Simmonds! You've been warned. Keep your filthy drug propaganda out of here. Right? Now. . . . Ten laps! At the double!

Peter: [*To audience*] Sue was waiting for us, when I finished.

Sue: You look better already, pet.

Peter: [*Collapsing*] You reckon?

Sue: Did you enjoy yourself?

Peter: Oh, yeah. . . . Fantastic.

Sue: Now, if you didn't you've got to tell us — say so, love. I don't want you ever to hide anything from me.

Peter: No.

Sue: Did you enjoy it. You really did, didn't you? Admit it.

Peter: You want to know the truth, then, Sue?

Sue: You've always got to tell me the truth, pet. I don't want it to be like your mam and dad. . . . Where the only thing they say to each other is pass the salt and vinegar.

Peter: Right, then, Sue. . . . It's bloody punishment. They have better laughs in Durham goal East Wing!

Sue: Now, Peter. It's not as bad as that, now, pet.

Peter: Bloody worse!

Sue: Peter . . . Jackie goes three nights a week. You go once a week, love.

Peter: You asked us to tell you the truth. I'm telling you . . . amn't I?

Sue: Well . . . the first few weeks . . . bound to be hard. . . .

It's just, you've let your body completely go, pet. . . . After a month or so . . .

Peter: Be bloody dead.

Sue: Peter, love. [*Fussing over him. Odd kiss*] It's just for your own good, pet. I want to look after you, properly, don't I? Your mother's not bothered, *how* you look! You want to have a nice, strong, lean manly body. . . . Don't you?

Peter: Do I? [*To audience*] Did I?

Sue: [*Arm in his*] Of course you do. . . . And you're going to have one, too. I know.

Peter: [*To audience*] Next thing she started on was stopping me tabs. That was Alfie, the camp commandant getting on to her. . . . Told her I'd never get anywhere till I stopped smoking.

Sue: I want you to enjoy life, pet . . . I love you. . . .

Peter: I *am* enjoying life. [*To audience*] I was too. If she'd bloody leave us alone!

Sue: All these drugs, Peter. They just take away the edge from enjoying everything. Even physical relationships.

Peter: [*To audience*] She's just started on the Pill, and this was her first week. She had to be on it a month or so before we could do anything. But she was getting ready. [*To* **Sue**] Physical relationships?

Sue: It just completely weakens the body . . . *physically*. You know what I mean, pet?

Peter: [*Looking down to check*] New one on me, that! [*To* **Sue**] Smoking? [*To audience*] Knew it sometimes goes for your *chest!*

Sue: Look at your dad . . . and your mam. . . . Like a kipper factory in your house! You've got to kind of wave away the smoke to see the telly.

Peter: Me dad's nearly fifty-five. . . . That's what it is. Nothing to do with tabs. [*To audience*] I don't *think* it was. . . . Was it?

Sue: Charlie Chaplin had all his powers till he was seventy and over. . . .

Peter: [*To audience*] How did she know that? [*To* **Sue**] How do you know that?

Sue: He had a baby when he was seventy-one.

Peter: Yeah. That's what his *lass* said! Getting us off smoking was only the beginning.

Sue: Peter . . . come here a minute. Sit on my knee, a minute, pet.

Peter: [*To audience*] Always did that when she wanted to get round us. [*To* **Sue**] Later.

Sue: Come on.

Peter: I'm all right here.

Sue: Peter. [*He gives in. Sits on her knee*]

Sue: [*Stroking his hair*] I love you.

Peter: I love you.

Sue: I want you to be happy, pet.

Peter: I am, man. [*To audience*] I wish she'd stop bloody saying that!

Sue: You're not really, I know. A person like you couldn't be really happy in that factory. It's not for you, Peter. I know. Deep down. You're not really happy there.

Peter: [*To audience*] Was I not?

Sue: You could be anything. I know. You've got the intelligence. An accountant. Or a traveller. Or even a teacher.

Peter: Sue, do you still love us? [*To audience*] I got very upset when she started talking like that. [*To* **Sue**] I mean. You're not going to leave us, are you?

Sue: I'm not going to leave you, pet? I love you . . . I just want you to make something out of yourself. I couldn't stand thinking of you stuck at a machine day in day out, watching cigarettes pouring out.

Peter: I'm on the *packing* machines. I told you. I don't watch them coming *out.*

Sue: Listen, pet. You're a good driver, aren't you? I'll speak to my boss. Securicor's always looking for good, reliable people. That can be trusted. That's how they get all their staff. Recommendations.

Peter: Securicor?

Sue: I'll speak to the boss, in the morning.

Peter: I don't think I'd be much use against pay-roll gangs with sawn-off shotguns, Sue.

Sue: In the same job as me. Documents. You go all round Newcastle and Gateshead. Even Sunderland ... at times. Meeting all kinds of people. It's interesting, Peter. Some of the jobs you go on. You'd really enjoy it. I know.

Peter: So long as I don't have to carry a truncheon and people expect us to defend bags of fivers with me life.

Sue: I'm telling you, pet. You'd love it.

Peter: Would I?

Sue: I'll ask him in the morning. [*Cuddling him*] Listen. If you get the early shift, like me. We could have the afternoons off together. Be lovely having the afternoons off together when we're married, wouldn't it?

Peter: Cannie.

Sue: It's lovely in the afternoons. Especially on a cold, wet, winter's day.

Peter: Is it?

Sue: Wait and see.

Peter: [*To audience*] How did *she* know? ... I mean ... I didn't think about it at the time. But it makes you think, doesn't it? I wasn't mad about Securicor. But if it makes her happy. Trouble was, me mam wouldn't have it.

Mam: I'm not having it.

Dad: See what you want to do, son, is relax. People's got this idea they should be happy. Running around like mad all over the place. Flogging themselves to death trying to enjoy themselves.

Mam: In Securicor! What are you thinking about, son! You've a lovely, secure job in Wills. The manager thinks the world of you. A job for life. And throwing it all away to go to Securicor! Jimmie! She's trying to make him go into Securicor!

Dad: That's what I'm talking about, man. I know it's a waste of time talking to anybody. Nobody ever listens to you.

Peter: I'm listening to you Dad. [*To audience*] I was. Sometimes he came out with things that made you think, this time he was going to get somewhere. You know? Now I'm going to hear something that's going to get me really organized.

Dad: Talking about people being happy, son.

Mam: Have you heard what he's saying, Jimmie man. Our one and only lad. Risking his life every day. With bank robbers and criminals and IRA all over the place after him. Say something to the boy, man.

Dad: I'm telling him, amn't I, woman. [*To* **Peter**] You don't need to be happy, man. I'm talking from experience. Relax, son. Just say to yourself: 'People are not made to be happy.' Telling you. You'll have the time of yer life!

Mam: She's taking over the boy's life, man! Peter, pet. If you were in a job like that. My nerves would be up to high doh all day till you got back, imagining all the things that could be happening to you. I've seen them on the television. They throw tear gas and bombs and mow them down with machine guns . . . in a job like that.

Dad: I know I'm bloody wasting my breath talking to *you* or anybody else. At the same time. It passes the time of day, doesn't it? I mean. And if people live together in the same house and you take bread with them. You might as well *talk* to them, mightn't you?

Mam: Jimmie, man. I'm trying to have a serious discussion with the boy, for God's sake. Peter, pet, this a move that might ruin your whole life. Listen te yer mam, love.

Dad: I'm telling him, man. If he's doing it because he thinks it's going to make him happier. Forget it! People are not made to be happy, son. Especially people like us.

Mam: He's doing it because that bloody bitch ordered him to do it, man. What are you talking about? He loves his job in Wills. Don't you, son?

Dad: If he's doing it because the lass told him to. That's a different question, altogether.

Mam: Look at him. He doesn't know where he is, just now. That rotten bitch has got him, so he has to ask her if she thinks he should go to the nettie.

Dad: If he's doing it for the lass. We're into the question of freedom. That's another thing that's nowt to do with people. People aren't *made* to be free. Why should they? Look at me. I go down to the yard. Sit up there in me crane eight hours a day. Doesn't bother me. Doesn't bother anybody. . . .

Mam: Peter. It's no use listening to *him*. He doesn't know where the bloody hell he is.

Dad: I'm talking about him having to obey *somebody's* orders, man, amn't I? If you have to live with a woman, you've got to stand them dictating to you. Either he takes his orders from you or her. . . . It's up to him, isn't it. . . .

Mam: Will you stop interfering, and confusing the lad! . . . Here's 50p. Go down to the club, man. Peter. . . . Now listen to me. I am not having you dictated to. I'm not having it. You hear us. You are not leaving Wills! You hear us? . . . I'll tell her straight.

You wait till that bitch shows her face here. I'll sharp give her some home truths.

Peter: [*To audience*] Didn't have to wait long. She turned up five minutes later, to tell us I had an interview for Securicor Monday morning, etc.

Mam: [*Arms folded. In full battle order*] You're here, are you, miss?

Sue: I'm a bit early. [*Going to kiss* **Peter**]. You all right, pet?

Mam: [*Blocking her from him*] Leave my lad alone, just now, miss. Peter, go into the bedroom!

Dad: Don't be daft, man. . . . He's over twenty-one.

Mam: Now . . . you and I, Susan, have a few things to say to each other, haven't we?

Sue: Have we?

Dad: Now . . . I'll tell you something, Susan.

Mam: I thought I told *you* to go to the club. . . .

Dad: I'm going, woman. I'm just saying. You're not a bad lass, Susan. I've watched you. And as they go, nowadays. You're a cannie lass. Not that any of yer generation are all that up to much. There's something missing in all of you.

Mam: It's about time, miss, you and I came out into the open. I've watched the way you've been trying to control my boy. And I've to keep it in all these months for his sake.

Sue: If we're coming into the open, Mrs Simmonds. If that's what you want. You've dictated to Peter all his life. You've got him so that he doesn't know what he wants. He's no mind of his own at all.

Mam: Do you hear her? You hear the bitch. Are you going to stand there letting her insult me in my own house?

Dad: I'm saying. There's something missing in all of them. I know that's what every older generation's supposed to say about the younger one. But this time it's true. It's a fact. The same time. You're a canny lass. Between you and me. I've been meaning to say this all along. I cannot understand what you see in our Peter. Look at him, man.

Mam: For God's sake! . . . Will you shut yer stupid trap. I'm asking you. You filthy bitch, you. What do you mean by that. Saying I dictate to my own son. You take that—

Sue: Couldn't we not discuss this sensibly and calmly, Mrs Simmonds.

Mam: Don't call me Mrs Simmonds.

Sue: [*Taking Peter's arm*] Come on, Peter. We'd better leave your mother to calm down.

Mam: [*Shouting*] Don't tell me to calm down, miss! [*pulling* **Peter** *away from her*] I am perfectly calm and collected! I want just a word with you. That's all. . . .

Sue: Are you coming, Peter?

Mam: I've been very patient with you, these last few months. I've held my peace and grinned and bared it. Haven't I, Jimmie?

Dad: You know what it is? I'll tell you what it is, Susan. Look at the lad.

Sue: I love him.

Dad: Yes. That's all right for a couple months, lass. A year at the most. That love game. I'm speaking te you like this, because I've taken te you. You're a cannie, straight, sensible lass, except where our lad's concerned. . . .

Mam: Will you stop bloody interfering, man. If ye can't talk sense, just shut yer mouth . . . man.

Dad: I'm saying that love game's all right for them lasses that go about with glazed eyes, with a transistor hanging from their ears, blasting out Radio One from morning to night. But for you and me, lass. . . . That love game. Fairy tales, isn't it, now?

Peter: I love her, Dad. [*To audience*] Didn't know what the bloody hell *he* was getting at, now.

Dad: Or him, Sue. All right for him. [*To Peter*] What you want is one of them transistor lasses, Peter. That's your type, son!

Mam: Are ye going te let me *speak*, man? . . . Have you done, like? Have ye run down yer only lad enough, now.

Dad: [*To Sue*] Look at me and her. What about that? That was a love match, wasn't it, Missus? And look where it's bloody got *us!*

Mam: I'll talk to you afterwards. You know well enough where it's got you. *You've* taken no hurt from it! How many times had you to ask us before I said 'yes'. Tell her that. You down on your knees getting us to take you.

Dad: I'm telling her, amn't I? That's exactly what I'm telling her. I know from bitter experience where love gets you.

Mam: Just you keep out of this. If that's all ye can say! [*To Sue*] Now. You listen, here, miss. It's no use listening to him. He doesn't know where the hell he is. He's never been a father to the boy. If he'd been a proper father to him, it might've been a different story. Peter is perfectly happy in Wills. It's a job in a million. And I am not letting anybody mess up his life and drag him into a dangerous job like Securicor! He's not leaving Wills. Ye hear us. Before you turned up, he was a happy, contented boy . . . people used to remark on it.

Sue: That's right . . . so's a bloody chicken in a battery chicken factory!

Mam: Don't you use bad language like that in my house, miss, if you please. If he's not good enough for you, working in Wills. You know what to do about it! . . . If you want to still go out with Peter. Let's hear no more about him changing his job . . . to suit you. Just leave the boy alone.

Sue: It's up to Peter, isn't it. What he wants.

Mam: That's right. Just leave him to do what he wants to do.

Sue: What do you want to do, then, Peter?

Mam: Go on, then Peter. Tell her straight. You want to stay on at Wills.

Sue: Will you let him speak for himself. [*To* **Peter**] You told me, pet. You fancied a job in Securicor, didn't you? Going around all over the place—

Mam: He's perfectly happy where he is. Tell her, Peter.

Sue: Will you let him speak for himself! Peter, love. You're going for that interview on Monday morning, aren't you? It's all arranged.

Peter: [*To audience*] Bloody stuck there. Between the two of them. Like in the films on telly about the jungle. Couple of lions, tearing this antelope in two. I mean. What do you say? I loved Sue. And I loved me mam. I was happy in Wills. I didn't want to drive all over Newcastle, in a big van wearing one of those sweaty leather helmets!

Mam: Come on, man. Tell her you're happy in Wills.

Sue: If that's what you really want to do, Peter, love. If you're happy ending your life in a battery chicken factory.

Peter: [*To audience*] I mean. What do you do in a situation like that, for God's sake?

Sue: Come on, Peter. What do you really want to do?

Peter: I love you, Sue.

Mam: She's not asking you that.

Peter: I do. I don't know. I don't know what I want to do. If you'd all bloody leave us alone for a bit. [*To audience*] Thought that was the best policy. Let everybody cool off. Not say either way. Best policy!

Sue: The best thing is to find out these things before it's too late, Peter.

Peter: [*To audience*] What things?

Sue: That's what engagements are for, aren't they? [*reaching for her ring, holding it out to him*] There you are. This is the best way for both of us.

Peter: Sue, man. I don't want the ring back.

Dad: Take it, man.

Peter: I don't want it back, man.

Dad: [*Taking it*] I'll take it, Sue. Give it to me.

Sue: I mean. It's better finding out now, isn't it, than after a couple of years when we've had kids and everything. Isn't it? We're just two different types, aren't we?

Mam: Quite right, Susan. You're taking a very sensible attitude.

Peter: Sue, man. I'll go to Securicor on Monday. I promise.

Mam: Don't be daft, man.

Peter: Sue . . . I'll go . . . I will.

Sue: [*Going*] I'll probably see you around.

Peter: [*Going after her*] Sue, man. [*To audience*] Followed her outside. I mean. What was she *on* about? We were all right till we got engaged, weren't we? [*To* **Sue**] Sue, man. Don't leave us. I love you.

Sue: You'll get over it, Peter. Better get back to your fish supper before it gets cold.

Peter: That was me mam, Sue. Honestly. First fish supper I've had all week. [*To audience*] That was what was getting her. Promised to lay off fish suppers for good. Putting pounds on us a week she reckoned. [*To* **Sue**] Honestly, Sue. . . . Ask me mam.

Sue: Peter, it's no use. We're too different . . . in our ways. Get yourself a nice girl in Wills. Be loads to suit you there. Be fighting for the rest of our lives, Peter. If you and me got married.

Peter: Me mam forgot, Sue, man. She didn't have anything in the house. So she went round for a fish supper.

Sue: I can't stand it, man. Watching you in that chicken factory. Can you bloody understand. All day at your machine in the chicken factory. Standing there. Thinking about what you're going to buy this week with your wages. Or what's on in the telly that night.

Peter: And *you*. I think about *you* a lot, too, man. I like buying things and watching telly. We go to the pictures, too, don't we? And the club. Don't we? [*To audience*] And then my bloody mam had to shout down from the window.

Mam: Will you come and finish your tea, Peter. Your chips are getting cold. Cost us sixty pence . . . that fish supper. Double chips.

Peter: [*To* **Sue**] Promise you, Sue, man. Never eat another chip in me life. [*To audience*] Switched off. Like you switch off your engine in the car. Not a spark.

Sue: [*Walking off*] I'll see you, Peter.

Peter: I love you, man! [*Going inside, to* **Mam**] I love her, mam. I bloody love her!

Dad: That's people, son. They never get what they want. Don't know most of the time what they want, anyway.

Peter: Mam, I love her.

Mam: She's no use to you, pet. Listen te yer mam.

Peter: I want her, for Christ's sake! I love her, mam. I bloody love her.

Mam: I'll tell you something, son. In a few weeks time, you'll bless the day you finished with that rotten bitch.

Peter: I love her . . . I want her. . . .

Mam: She's no use to you, son. Listen te yer mother. . . .

Peter: I want her, for Christ's sake.

Mam: Listen, son. You eat up your fish supper and have an
early night, pet. I'm telling you. You've done a good day's
job, tonight. Do you want some pickled cabbage with your
chips?

Peter: [*To audience*] Then I did a funny thing. I threw the bag
of fish and chips in me mam's face. [*To* **Mam**] Stuff yer rotten
fish and chips up your rotten arse! [*To audience*] I mean . . . I
never did anything like that in me life before. . . .

Mam: My God! God in heaven! What's happening to us?

Peter: Mam . . . I   didn't   mean   it. . . . It   just   kind   of—

Dad: Throwing good food at people like that, man!

Mam: It's all right, son. You're just upset. It's that rotten bitch.

Dad: [*Scraping up fish and chips*] Sixty p's worth of fish and
chips!

Peter: I didn't mean it, mam . . . [*To audience*] Bloody did! . . .
Had a right night, that bloody Saturday night. Up all night,
trying to work it out. Woke up about nine o'clock and heard
these two messing about making breakfast. Frying bacon. I
mean what do you do? Go downstairs and listen to these two
telling us this was the happiest day of me life. Sit around the
house all morning, watching telly, with me mam peeling potatoes and making Yorkshire pudding batter. . . . Go with me
Dad to the rotten club and listen to him going on about how
people have no future . . . world's going to end up being taken
over by animals. Or other bloody rubbish like that. I mean . . .
that was going to be me life everyday, now, without Sue. On
and on and bloody on. Couldn't even stand Wills, now. . . . Maybe there *was* something wrong working there. Looked out the
window. Started to bloody drizzle, now on top of everything
else. Bugger it. Bloody sick. I mean. Not one thing to look
forward to, now. She's finished with us. Bloody stick in
Byker her with me rotten Mam and Dad the rest of me life.

Mam: [*From downstairs*] Peter, pet. Are ye coming down for yer breakfast. I've a lovely cut of side bacon for you and two eggs.

Peter: [*To audience*] See what I bloody mean! Put on me jacket and walked out the house. Made straight for the river. Had a look at the Swing Bridge but I didn't think it was right. Bit low and there was the man in the cabin on top, working it. Had a look at the High Level. But there was too many people about. So I went back to the George the Fifth.

Policeman: [*With ladder*] Make way, please. Clear the road. [*Places ladder against bridge*] Now, listen, son. I'm going to stick this ladder here. Not going to do anything else. And if you feel like coming down. Fair enough. It's there, isn't it?

TV Man: I wonder if we mightn't get a better shot from the quayside using a zoom if he's going to jump.

Mam: God in heaven. Is he going to jump? Do you think he's going to jump?

TV Man: Apart from anything else. If it comes to it. And Peter does jump ... it'll give all these other kids who might be thinking negatively like him, a real jolt, won't it, Mrs Simmonds. He won't have jumped in vain. You see what I'm getting at?

Policeman: But there's every chance that he's not going to, isn't there?

Mam: [*To Policeman*] Do *you* think he's going to jump? Jimmie ... will you do something, man. The boy's going to jump.

Dad: He's got a ladder, hasn't he? What can I bloody do, man! Peter, man. Come on down, man. I want me bloody dinner, son. You've made yer point.

Mam: [*To Policeman*] You see if you can make him, constable. Do they not give you special training for cases like that. He's going to jump! He's going to jump into that filthy, cold, black—

Policeman: He's got his ladder, now, you see, missus. [*To* **Peter**] Tell you what, lad. We'll move back. Right. Everybody move back, now. There you are, son. We're not going to do anything. If you feel like coming down . . . fair enough . . . it's up to you. See . . . if you've got a good back, lad. Makes all the difference in the world, doesn't it?

TV Man: Like Irving Berlin says . . . Peter . . . 'Count Your Blessings'.

Policeman: That's it . . . from *Rose Marie*. . . . [*Sings* Count Your Blessings]

Peter: [*To audience*] See what I mean. . . . Everything was going great till then. Could've just come down . . . no bother . . . I mean . . . I'd had my say . . . and the ladder was there. . . . Could've just climbed down when just at that minute another police car turns up. Doors open and out steps Sue.

Mam: You keep away from my boy, you rotten cow! You've done enough damage, filthy bitch! Had away te hell! [*Conscious of the return of the* **TV Man**] You haven't had your camera on, just now, have you. . . . It was just the heat of—

TV Man: Waiting for more film.

Mam: Ye hear us, ye bitch, you! Piss of back te yer Benwell Shithouse!

Sue: Peter. . . .

Mam: [*To* **Sue**] Will you take a talking to, you bitch, you! [*Going to attack her*]

Policeman: Ladies . . . ladies. . . . Steady . . . now. Take it easy. . . .

Dad: [*To crowd*] It's all right. . . . It's just a family matter.

Sue: Will you please let me get to Peter, Mrs Simmonds!

Mam: You bloody try, miss! [*To crowd*] That's the rotten bitch who's ruined my poor boy's life! You see what you've done, you filthy sex-maniac cow! [*Unable to control herself any longer, starts attacking her*]

Policeman: Ladies . . . calm down, now . . . I have to warn you.

Peter: There they were . . . lashing into each other . . . tearing each other's hair out . . . when me Dad said the most sensible thing in his life.

Dad: Madge, man! You're getting yourself into a right bloody mess there for them cameras!

Mam: [*Immediately breaking off*] I'm not worried about the cameras!

Sue: Peter . . . listen to me.

Mam: [*To* **Samaritan**] Have you a comb or something. . . . Look at what that bitch has done to me hair!

Sue: Come on down, pet. I didn't realize your feelings for us were so strong. Come on, love. We'll work out something together.

Policeman: There you are, Peter. Everything's worked out all right, now, hasn't it?

Peter: See what I mean . . . I'm up there, looking down at Sue. She was in a right mess, after me mam had done with her. Nose running. Hair all over the place. Mascara running and making her eyes look funny.

Sue: Please, Peter. I love you. I didn't realize your love for me was so deep.

Peter: Went right off her there and then. I mean. . . .

Sue: Listen, Peter. I'm not going to let them away with it. Keeping you caged in that horrible factory. I'm going to really fight for you. Come on down, love. I love you. I really do. We'll fight them together. . . .

Peter: [*To audience*] See what I mean. Still getting on to us. Worse than ever. Wouldn't even leave us alone on the bridge.

Sue: I just gave in too easy, last night, Peter. We'll work it out together. I mean the Securicor's just a start. . . . Just to get you out of that battery chicken factory. . . .

Policeman: Want us to hold the ladder steady for you, son.

Sue: And I'll tell you what, love. We'll get a flat somewhere . . . and get married. We'll start looking tomorrow. I'll get a *Journal* first thing in the morning. Once we're on our own together. We'll be fine, won't we?

Policeman: Come on, son. That's all yer wishes granted, isn't it? And ye've a good back on top of everything else. Just reach out for the ladder. Careful, now.

Sue: Peter, love. Are you coming to me? Come on, pet. . . .

Peter: [*To audience*] What do you do in a situation like that? *Right* bloody mess, now! If I went down, I'd have to go back to Sue. Gone right off her in these last five minutes. . . . Me mam's right. You should never marry the first lass ye see. Something in what people say about always listening te yer mam, isn't there? I mean. . . . To be lumbered with that misery down there. Nagging at us night and day . . . with her runny nose. . . .

Sue: Are you coming down, love?

Peter: Yer nose is running.

Mam: Come on, Peter. We'll all go home for dinner, love. I've a lovely joint of pork in the oven. Crackling melt in your mouth.

Peter: [*To audience*] Bloody famished, too. . . . Pork.

Policeman: Just reach out for the ladder, son. Careful. . . .

Peter: I was just giving in. I mean, what could I do. I couldn't stay up there for ever. Now she'd come back to us again. So I kind of turned round to reach the ladder. And God or somebody saved us.

Man: My God! I think he's going to jump!

Dad: Peter, man!

Sue: Peter!

Samaritan: Don't say anything. . . .

Peter: [*To audience*] I bloody fell off!

Mam: My God! He's jumped! Oh . . . dear Jesus in heaven!
. . . The boy's jumped. . . . Save him. Somebody. For God's
sake. Jimmie.

Peter: [*To audience*] Fell right into the river . . . bloody stink.
. . . Like all the shithouses in Newcastle has just pulled their
plugs! But no doubt about it . . . God was looking after us.
. . . Hardly hit the water, when the police were pulling us into
the police launch. . . .

Lass: Listen . . . you talking about roast pork's made us hungry.
. . . Come on . . . we'll go down to Bell's for a fish supper.

Peter: Wouldn't mind a fish supper. . . . Yeah . . . wouldn't
mind a fish supper. [*To audience*] Same day. Me mam went
over to her mam's . . . Told her it was all finished. . . . [*To
audience*] Minute I got·her off me back, I really settled down
at Wills. Having the time of me life, now. I bought one of
them new Datsuns and one of these hi-fi centres, the same
week. Me mam said it would take me mind off her. Took a
couple of days before we get me Dad to go into a Jap car. . . .
Time we got him to Tynemouth, he said, if the world's coming
to an end, ye might as well see it out in a reliable car. Just now,
we're trying to get a new working system in Wills. Half an hour
on, half an hour off. Think we're going to win, too. I mean.
It's a smashing job, isn't it? And these days. Bloody lucky to
be *working*, aren't you?

Lass: [*Taking his hand, pulling him out of club*] Come on.
That clown's going to sing again. [*The band strikes up into*
Some Enchanted Evening. **Lass** *stops for a moment*] Oh
. . . I've left me transistor on the table. [*Going for it*]

Peter: Cannie set. . . .

Lass: Smashing tone. Put it on when we get out of here....
[*The* **Singer** *launches into song. The* **Lass** *stops for a moment in the doorway*] Hear what they're singing.

Peter: Yeah....

Singer: 'Some Enchanted Evening.
You may see a stranger.
You may see a stranger
Across a crowded room....'

Lass: There'll always be romance, won't there ... Do you not think so....

Peter: [*As they go*] Yeah ... there will.... You're right....

Singer: 'You may hear her laughing.
Across a crowded room.
And somehow you know.
You know even then.
That some day you'll see her,
Again and again....'

The End

The Filleting Machine

Tom Hadaway

Characters

Ma, in her fifties
Da, also in his fifties
Davy, 15, their eldest son
Alice, 14, their eldest daughter

First performed on BBC Television in the 'Full House' series on 17 March 1973

The Filleting Machine

Scene: **A council house living room, with kitchen off stage.** *The house is on the Ridges estate, North Shields. The area is a depressed enclave of poor whites who have been slum-cleared from the fish dock district. In the distance, the raucous strident sound of children in the battlefield of the street can be heard.* **Ma** *is preparing a meal.* **Alice** *calls from offstage.*

Alice: Mother! Mother!

Ma: Hellow!

[*The door opens and* **Alice** *comes bursting in*]

Alice: The bairn's covered wi' baked beans, an' tea leaves.

Ma: Gawd almighty!

Alice: Tattie peelin's, an allsorts reet in the pram.

Ma: That dorty buggar upstairs. Tossin' his rubbish oot the winder.

Alice: It's all claggy. Yuk! [*She limps across the room. One of her legs is bandaged*]

Ma: Tryin' ti get the dinner on. An' look at the state o' that bandage. Fresh on this mornin'. Ye'll end up with it septic.

Alice: Better take a flannel, the pram's *lathered.*

[**Ma** *snatches a cloth from a drying line*]

Ma: Take that buggar a piece o' me mind [*She leaves and we hear her voice offstage, receding*] Ye great lazy good for nowt. Ye've got the place covered wi' yor filth.

[**Alice** *switches on her transistor radio. Music. She wanders over to the window to listen to the altercation outside*]

Aye! thor's none so deef as doesn't want ti hear. Fancy hevin' ti live under dorty buggars like you.

[**Alice** *wanders back to a chair, sits and takes up a comic*]

Ye want bloody sortin' out.

[*The kitchen door opens and* **Davy** *comes cautiously in. He is dressed in a wind jacket and rubber boots*]

Alice: Hi, Davy!

Davy: What's up?

Alice: Upstairs! Covered the little'n wi' shit.

Davy: Oh! [*He begins to take off his jacket.* **Alice** *studies him*]

Alice: Where you been?

Davy: Doon by.

Alice: On the fish quay?

Davy: So what?

Alice: Get yor hammers if she finds out. Better hide them wellies.

[**Davy** *considers confiding a secret. He stands up holding his boots*]

Davy: Gotta job.

Alice: Gotta what?

Davy: Gotta job.

Alice: On the fish quay?

Davy: Start o' Monday.

Alice: Ye haven't?

Davy: Wanna bet?

Alice: Eee! what ye ganna tell Ma?

Davy: [*Doubtful*] Jus' tell her.

Alice: She'll gan crackers.

Davy: Who cares?

Alice: She'll lose hor blob.

Davy: [*Irritated*] Alreet! Alreet!

Alice: What aboot yor interview for the Town Clerk's?

Davy: [*Contemptuous*] Oh! that! That's had it.

Alice: Eee! She'll gan daft.

[*Offstage* Ma *can be heard returning*]

Ma: Bloody wasters.

Alice: She's comin!

Ma: Neither work nor want.

[*At the sound of his mother,* Davy *panics, grabs his jacket and boots and prepares to bolt into the kitchen*]

Davy: Now you shut yor gob, Alice, or A'll shut it for ye.

Alice: Push off.

[Davy *retreats into the kitchen.* Alice *turns up the radio and a second later* Ma *comes in through the main door*]

Ma: A dunno. He'll put nowt in that bin. 'Cept a Friday, when he's passin' it on the way ti the social security. Ye bugs. Likes o' them pickin' up a ticket. Alice! Torn that blarin' thing off. [**Ma** *switches the radio off*] One row after another. [*From the kitchen comes the sound of a tap running.* **Ma** *looks in the direction of the sound*] Is there somebody out there? Davy? Davy? Is that you son? [*She pauses, then shouting*] Davy!

Davy: Aye, ma! [**Davy** *comes in. He pushes past his mother, snatches the comic from his sister and sits*]

Ma: Come on, bonny lad, it's past five o'clock. [*She sniffs inquiringly in the air*] Yor da wi' ye?

Davy: No, ma.

Ma: S'funny, could've swore A smelled him.

Davy: Gotta lock in. Doon at Charlie's.

Ma: [*Outraged*] Gotta what? Has he had you in the boozer?

Davy: Aw, ma! A'm owny fifteen.

Ma: An yor a big fifteen, an' yor da's a big idiot. Now come on, A want the truth.

Davy: Jus' seen him gannin' in with his mates. Ye knaa! Chopper, Sainty, Danny Mac. Charlie gi' them a lock in.

Ma: Mates! Bloody wasters more like it. Dissolvin' thor brains wi' broon ale. Three card brag 'till yon time. They'll take him ti the cleaners. Another short week. [*Suspiciously,* **Ma** *sniffs again. She comes directly over to* **Davy** *and bends over him*] Poo! It's you. It's you, isn't it? Ye smell like a gut barrel. No wonder A thought yor father was in the hoose.

Davy: Aw, ma.

Ma: Ye've been doon on that quay, haven't ye?

Davy: Ma!

Ma: Now come on, A want no lies.

Davy: Just gi' me da a hand ti wash a few boxes oot. Gettim a quick finish.

Ma: A'll finish him.

Davy: Bob Wilson give's a quid.

Ma: Nivvor mind aboot Bob Wilson. Ye'll get the smell o' fish on ye. Gans right thro' yor claes, into yor skin, an' thor's no gettin' rid of it.

Davy: Ma!

Ma: Now, Davy, A've telled ye. [*She goes to the mantelpiece to take a letter from an ornament. While her back is turned* **Alice** *gestures to* **Davy** *urging him to tell his Ma about the job.* **Davy** *summons up his courage*]

Davy: Ma! When A was on the quay. . . .

Ma: Now look, son, forget about the quay. Ye've got that interview next week. [*She demonstrates the letter*] This is your chance in life. Ye've got yor O-levels. Davy, it's yor chance ti mix wi better people.

Davy: What's better aboot them?

Ma: Well, maybe thor no better than us son, but thor not on casual. They've got positions. Davy it's yor place on the bus. Don't end up like yor da.

Davy: Nowt wrong wi' me da.

Ma: Nowt wrong wi' donkeys, but the' divven let them on busses.

Davy: Sooner hev me da, than any o' them in the Toon Clerk's. All paper hankies for snot rags.

Ma: Davy! Divven be si coarse.

Davy: Ma, hev ye seen them? Stuck in thor desks. No proper winders ti look out. All that frosty glass, like the' hev in bogs. Pathetic! Sittin' pretendin' ti be doin' summick important. All the time, starin' sideways, ti see who's comin', an' gannin', wishin' it was thorselves. Might as well be at skule.

Ma: School, Davy. School, not skule.

Davy: All right! School, skule, what's the difference?

Ma: A'll tell ye what the difference is. It's when the' go home at night. Thor not comin' ti the Ridges estate. No, they're livin' where flowers has the chance o' growin' , an' a young laddie like you isn't just summick the polis has ti keep an eye on. Where ye can hev respect, an' yor own front door, an nee female welfare supervisor demandin' ti be in, ti cut yor pride off at the knees. Aye, by God, that's the dif'rence. [*Pause. She moves across to the window to glance out*] Aye, an' when the' hang thor washin' oot in the mornin', it's still there at dinner time.

Davy: Ma, yor a patter merchant. Should hev ye on the tele.

Ma: Ridges estate! What are wi? Just a joke. Ridges estate! Them that keeps thor coals in the bath. Go to a store for credit. Ridges estate? The' don't want ti know. Go for a decent job. Ridges estate? No chance.

Davy: How come A got that interview then?

Ma: That proves yor somethin' special, Davy. Somebody seen ye were dif'rent. Somebody's took a fancy ti ye.

Davy: Hold on, ma. Don't want nobody fancyin' us.

Ma: Son, it's yor chance in life. Ye don't want a dead end job. Toss away all your education. All that study. Don't let yourself down Davy, an' don't let me down.

Davy: Ma, yor not on. Things isn't like that now.

Ma: Like what?

Davy: Gettin' a good job in an office. Security, all that jazz. That went out wi' trams. Thor's better money on the docks.

Ma: Aye, an' how long will that last? Thor clawin' each other's back now, for a share o' the meat.

Davy: A can get twenty pound a week startin' money on the quay.

Ma: Little apples, Davy. That's yor da talkin', an' it's little apples.

Davy: An' extras.

Ma: What extras?

Davy: A bit fiddle.

Ma: [*Outraged*] Fiddle! What's a laddie like you talkin' about fiddle?

Davy: Nowt wrong wi' fiddle. Not like pinchin', it's just . . . fiddle. Da says every job on the quay has ti have a fiddle, or the' cannot keep the men.

Ma: Well, it sounds more like Mantovani's bloody orchestra ti me.

Davy: Aw, ma!

Ma: Now look, A'm havin' no argument. You were brought up ti touch nothin' that doesn't belong ye. Yor keepin' away from it. The fish quay is nowt but the home o' the forty thieves, an' A nivvor brought ye into the world ti be a fiddler.

[*Offstage,* **Da** *can be heard returning. He is a robust, friendly man, only aggressive when frustrated. Heavy with drink, he is singing. His pocket bulges with a bottle of brown ale and with his filleting knife wrapped in a cloth. The sleeves of his jacket are sawn off at the elbows, in the manner of all fish filleters, to keep them from dipping in the trough*]

Da: [*Offstage*] 'It's not unusual ti be loved by anyone, da, dee dee da.'

Ma: Gawd! an' here comes the forst violin.

Da: 'Not unusual, ti be loved by anyone, an' if ye. . . . '

[*The door opens and* **Da** *enters. He resonantly belches*]

Ma: That's lovely! Lovely A must say. Gi yor family the benefit o' yor company.

Da: [*Smiling with the satisfaction of the belch*] That's me. That's yor da. Why give it away ti strangers. [*He advances on* **Ma**. *Takes hold of her in a clumsy embrace. Forces her to dance. Sings*] 'Stranger in the night, da, da, dee dee da, strangers in the night'.

Ma: [*Forcing herself free*] Gerroff ye great puddin'. [*She goes off into the kitchen.* **Da** *takes off his jacket, puts it round the back of his chair and plants his bottle of brown ale on the table*]

Da: Puttin' that kettle on or what?

Ma: [*Offstage*] A'm puttin' the kettle on.

Da: Worra woman. Hellow Davy! That's my bonny lad. [*Ruffles his son's hair*] All right, son?

Davy: All right, da.

Da: [*Lowering his voice*] Hey! see them haddocks we were cuttin'. Eh? [*He demonstrates with his hands an approximate eight-inch length*] A says ti Bob Wilson, what di ye call these? he says 'Haddocks'. A says, 'Haddocks, ye mean dog's dicks.' A'm no kiddin' the' were no bigger'n dog's dicks.

[**Ma** *comes back in carrying a teapot, just in time to catch the obscenity of the remark*]

Ma: Do you hev ti use language like that an' yor own bit lassie sittin' there?

Da: Ooo! listen sanctimonious! Hey! there's a big word eh? Sang titty monious. Hey, ma, yor all right, till you get sang titty monious.

Ma: Gawd! [*She moves back into the kitchen. From this point onwards she goes back and forward from living room to kitchen laying the table*]

Da: Hellow, Alice. [*He leans over and cuddles her*] My little lass. [*He goes and looks in the sideboard drawer for a bottle opener*] My little stay-all-day-in-the-house Alice. All right, pet?

Ma: She stays in all day, 'cos she's given up fightin' sixty other bairns for a share o' the street.

Da: All right, ma. All right. A'm just sayin' hellow!

Ma: Have ye seen hor leg? Are ye bothered? Twelve stitches in, from the raggy end of a bottle.

Da: A know. A know! Still! She's got ti learn ti stick up for horsel'. [*To* Alice] You stick up for yorsel', pet. Fightin's natural, an' us is a fightin' family. Wi nivvor give up. Nivvor! You show 'em. [*He sits*]

Ma: Huh!

Da: A telled ye what General Montgomery sayed to us.

Ma: Not that again. [*She disappears into the kitchen*]

Da: [*Rising up*] General Montgomery [*Calling out to* Ma] personally ti me. [*To the kids*] S'fact! Standin' as near ti me as you are now. Ganna be this big do on, oot in the desert, y'know. Well, all the top brass was round ti gi' the lads a clap on the back. 'Corporal Rutter, 9268754, Royal Northumberland Fusiliers, sor.' Montgomery says, 'Kerprel', 'Kerprel', 'e says. 'Course he had this funny way o' taalkin', 'cos he's Irish y'know. 'Kerprel,' 'e says, 'You'se Geordies is fighters.' That's what 'e says, 'Fighters'. That was the famous general, Sir Bernadette Montgomery. Give wi all fifty tabs a piece. Couldn't smoke 'em. Bloody horrible. Owld bastard. But 'Fighters', pet, that what 'e sayed. So you show them Alice. Anyhow Ma, where's the rest o' the bairns? [Ma *returns*]

Ma: One in the pram ootside, ye probably fell ower hor withoot noticin'.

Da: Now, ma, canny on. No rows eh? We want no rows.

Ma: What di ye want? A roll call? Yor other three's out roamin' the railway. In the hands o' God, or the neighbours, whichever's the worst.

Da: Well, the bloody railway! They've never mended that fence. Not since the bairns took it down for Guy Fawkes. But look pet, A'm home for a bit o' peace an quiet. So let's have no rows, eh? That grub comin' or what?

Ma: [*Vehemently*] It's comin'. [*She leaves.* **Da** *pours himself the beer. There is a pause*]

Da: That's my Davy. All right, son. Yor a good'n. Hey, no kiddin', ye did yor da proud this mornin'. [**Ma** *comes in to catch the comment*] Oooo' sorry. [*Absurd gesture of secrecy*] Nuff sed!

Davy: S' all right, da. She knows A was on the quay.

Ma: Yor encouragin' him to go down there.

Da: Me?

Ma: Yes, you.

Da: Not me.

Ma: Fine example you are.

Da: Ma, A've telled ye. That laddie's got his own mind ti make up. He'll do what he wants ti do, and gan where he wants ti gan.

Ma: He's goin' for that interview.

Da: What interview?

Ma: Ye know fine well what interview. The Town Clerk's.

Da: The [*Scornfully*] Toon Clerk's.

Ma: Yes, the Toon Clerk's an' he's goin' for that interview.

Da: Ye've sayed that already.

[*She goes back into the kitchen making a decisive clatter of crockery*]

Da: [*Calling after her*] Ma, wor Davy's a sunshine lad. Y'know.

'E likes it oot in the fresh air, where the seagulls is flying roond. Huh', thor's no bloody seagulls in the toon clerk's.

Ma: [Offstage] 'Course thor's not, ye dope. What would the' be wantin' wi seagulls. Dirty, shitty things.

Da: [*Taken aback by the vehemence*] That grub comin', or what.

Ma: [*Offstage*] A've telled ye it's comin'.

Da: So's Chris'mas.

Ma: Alice come here, give's a hand.

[**Alice** *goes through to the kitchen to help bring in the plates of food*]

Da: [*To* **Davy**] Tell ye what. She'll have you in a bowler hat, wi' stripey pants.

Davy: Not me.

Da: Gi' yor mates a laugh.

Davey: Not likely.

Da: Toon Clerk's! Call that work? Ye bugs! Sittin' on thor backsides all day, pushin' a pen. Work! Hey! see what me an big Mutt lifted on the Grimsby wagon, eh? Ten ton! Ten bloody ton! Box, by box. None o' yor fancy fork lifts. Hundredweight, by hundredweight. Aye, an' the rain beatin' on wi. Now, that's what ye call work. Not a writer born, can write that down.

Ma: [*Offstage*] What ye sayin' to him?

Da: [*Calling back*] Trouble we' you, ma, ye place too much store on education. Yor tryin' ti be upstairs, an' doonstairs at the same time. An' what di ye get? Stuck on the landin'.

[**Davy** *and* **Da** *enjoy the joke.* **Ma** *comes in with the food and they all gather at the table.* **Ma** *plants* **Da's** *plateful savagely in front of him*]

Ma: Just fill yor gob wi' chips, an' let's have the biggest relief since Dunkirk. That bairn's goin' ti make use o' his education.

Da: Education!

Ma: Alice! Davy! Sit down, get yor grub.

Da: A'll tell ye somethin' about education. [*He speaks between mouthfuls of food*] It's no good ti the workin' class. Thor's two kinds of education. The kind the give ti us, and the kind the keep for thorselves. An' the kind the give ti us, yor better off withoot.

Ma: What do you know about education?

Da: Don't talk ti me about education.

Ma: What would be the point?

Da: Listen, what di ye think the idea is? So's we can better worselves? Don't kid on. Listen, the idea of education, is ti make the likes of us, useful ti the buggars that's gettin' the money. Education! Education don't make the job fit you. Education makes you fit the job. Listen, them desks in the Toon Clerk's was there long before he was born.

Ma: Jus' gerron wi' yor dinners, take no notice.

Da: Eh? What did ye say? Take no notice. . . . Don't you tell them ti take no notice o' me. [*Everyone stops eating. She has pushed* **Da** *too far*] There's a fine. . . . What ye mean, tellin' them that, eh? [*Shouting, half-rising and pointing his finger at* **Ma**] Don't you bloody tell them ti take no notice o' me. What a thing ti say. A'm tellin' them summick important. Don't you tell them ti take no notice o' me.

[*There is a stunned silence.* **Da** *sits and moodily begins to eat. He looks up at them*]

Da: All right! All right! Gerron wi' yor dinners. Education! Puts ye at a desk, or on a machine, an' that's what's wrong wi' this country. Too many machines, an' too many in bloody offices.

[*They resume eating. He speaks to his son*] Tell ye what, put me on a machine once. Aye! one o' them fork lift trucks. Hey' laugh. Well A could manage it all right. No bother. Switch it on. Into gear! Giddup! A went off along the factory floor . . . an' strite thro' the bloody office. [**Davy** *and* **Da** *and* **Alice** *laugh.* **Ma** *doesn't think it's funny*] Hey', that fettled them. A says . . . A says, 'A'm sorry, but A don't think A've quite got the hang of it.' Eeeee! ye bugs, laugh! 'Gerris cards.' 'Gerrim out.' But what A'm tryin' to tell ye, son, the laddie that's drivin' that truck now, what's he pickin' up, eh? A mankey thirty-five pound fifty. Why, it's washers. Look, look, A'll show ye. [**Da** *rises up and fishes into his hip pocket. He brings out a roll of money*] See that. See that handful. Sixty-four quid. Eh? How's that? Casual! In the hand! Sixty-four quid. That's what yor da picked up this week. Wi no education, son, ye might be no good ti nobody but yorsel', but it leaves ye we' no choice but ti get on. [**Da** *reaches round for his jacket. He removes his filleting knife from the pocket and unrolls the cloth covering it*]

Da: Look, A'll show ye. There ye are. That's all ye need, a good filleting knife. That's the instrument. Carve yorsel' a career.

Ma: What di ye want, bringing a wicked thing like that here.

Da: That's how ye cut 'em. [*He demonstrates the filleting of a fish*]

Ma: Put it down

Da: Poetry in motion. All hand cut, an' nothin' but the best.

Ma: Put it away.

Da: A mean it's a simple thing a knife. Eh? But what was ever invented that's more effective.

Ma: Will ye put it away.

[*Suddenly and alarmingly* **Da**'s *temper changes. The kids are frightened. The knife has the appearance of a dagger*]

Da: Will you shut yor silly hole. Shurrup! Shurrup! A'm talkin' ti them. Tryin' ti tell them somethin'. Ye's never listen to us, none o' ye.

Davy: A really fancy the inshore fishin' da, if A could get. . . .

Da: You as well, shurrup! Never bloody listen. That's another thing about education, gettin' thaem that's had it to shurrup. [**Davy** *gets up from his chair and walks away from his father.* **Da** *watches him go and lumbers unsteadily after him*] Now look Davy! . . . Son! Don't you walk away from me. [**Davy** *slumps into the big easy chair*] 'Cos A'm tellin' ye. . . . [**Davy** *ignores his father.* **Da** *attempts to rationalize*] Look, A sayed there was two kinds of education. Aye, well there's another sort of education, an' it's the sort ye get for yorsel'. Look! Look! [*It's almost as though he would embrace his son*] Bob Wilson! Take Bob Wilson! Y'know Bob. Eh? Comes cryin' ti me. Right? Got fifty boxes on his hands, right? Y'know, cod, haddock, plaice, what have ye. Right? How much Bob? How much? Fifty pence a box? Not on. Not on Bob. Sixty pence a box. Seventy pence a box. Ye want them filleted? Eighty pence a box. He's over a barrel, see? A squeeze the sod. A've got this. [*He brandishes the knife*] Aye, an' A can use it. A'm a skilled man. The' need me. Hev knife, will travel, an' thor's no arguin' wi' the uneducated. [*He goes back to the table and picks up the roll of notes*] Look son, look. Sixty-four quid. Not bad eh? If you can do like yor da, son, we'll be rollin'. [*He throws the roll of notes over to* **Ma**. *She pushes them away from her*]

Ma: Aye, an' where's yor sixty-four quids on the lay off weeks. When thor's no fish comin' in. What about the weeks wi' nowt?

Da: Woman! It's the rough we' the smooth.

Ma: Yor brains is locked behind iron bars. It's not a matter o' money.

[**Da** *furiously sweeps the money and half the table crockery onto the floor*]

Da: Ivvorythin's a matter o' money. Ivvorythin's a matter o' money.

[**Davy** *leaps to his feet*]

Davy: Don't da. Don't.

Ma: Ye great destructive beast. It's a matter o' livin' like people, not animals. Alice, away ootside, an' mind that bairn.

[**Alice** *scatters out of the room*]

Da: What's the matter, is the money not good enough for ye?

Ma: No, it's not.

Da: What more di ye want?

Davy: Don't, man, da. Don't.

Da: Shurrup. What more di ye want?

Ma: A'll tell ye what A want. A want the bairns brought up decent, an' not hearin' their mother shoutin' blue murder ti the neighbours every Saturday night.

Da: Gerraway ti hell. Stuffin' their heads wi' that rubbish. An' what difference would it make to us where wi lived? An' di ye think the wives in posh houses don't shout blue murder. Aye, maybes the' do it quieter, 'cos they've been educated ti be polite. An' if the neighbours heard them, they'd be ower polite ti listen.

[*During* **Da's** *speech* **Ma** *has begun to pick up the scattered debris from the floor*]

Davy: Da!

Da: Leastways ye've always got that fanny Ann from over the path ti come round slaverin' sympathy. [*Mocking*] 'What's the matter pet, has he been beltin' ye?' 'Is 'e away doon ti Charlie's again.' 'Eee poor soul, what ye have ti put up with.'

Davy: Da, lay off.

Da: It makes ye bloody sick. [*Thumps the table*] Us is born, an' bred in this Ridges estate, an' thor's no changin' that. An' thor's no changin' us. [*To* **Davy**] An' the sooner she gets the daft ideas out of hor heed the better. [*Closes up on* **Ma**] Look! Ye want that laddie ti better hisself, eh? That what ye want? Well let him go where the money is.

Ma: You, ye pull everythin' down ti your level.

Da: An' you. You! Ye'd turn me own bairns against us.

Davy: Da, man, leave it be.

Da: Turn me own bairns against us. 'Cos ye haven't the sense ti be content with what ye have.

Ma: Be content with what A have.

Da: Yes.

Ma: What is it A've got? Go on, tell us.

Da: Ye've a bloody roof over yor heed for a start.

Ma: A've ti be greateful for that. Is it all right livin', an behavin' like pigs, as long as w'are dry pigs.

Da: Yor mother an' father were glad of a roof over thor head.

Ma: Aye, me mother an' father come out o' the low street. Yes, the' were slum clearance, but the' were happy.

Da: [*With contempt*] Happy!

Ma: Yes, happy! That's somethin' thor's no room for here. Like thor's no room for hope, an' no room for love.

Da: Love! [*As though it were a sick word*] Ye great soft bitch. What's that got ti do with it?

Davy: Don't, da.

Ma: Aye, A'm a soft bitch. Found that out the night A married you, an' yor mates carried ye upstairs to us.

Da: A've given ye six bairns.

Ma: Yes, mevves yor not fit ti drive a fork lift truck but thor's one job ye proved yorsel' on.

Da: That's right, get yor bloody joke in.

Ma: It's no joke. But yor not top o' the league. Upstairs has given his soft bitch nine, next door has got eight, and the soft bitch ower the path has ten up ti now.

Da: What's that got ti do wi' me, ye daft bat?

Ma: It's what A'm sayin', yor not responsible. Ye've no more talent that what it takes ti fillet a fish, but yor allowed ti run yor own private orphanage, an' ye've got it that crowded, thor queuein' for the netty.

[*Infuriated and still wielding the knife,* **Da** *lunges at* **Ma**]

Da: Ye talk a load o' rubbish.

[**Davy** *darts across, grabs his father by the arm and hangs on fiercely*]

Davy: Da! Da!

Da: Nowt but a load o' rotten rubbish. All the time, rubbish! rubbish! [*He tries to break free of* **Davy**]

Davy: Da! A've gotta job! A've gotta job, da.

[**Da** *looks at* **Davy** *uncomprehendingly*]

Da: What you talkin' about. Job! Job! What job! [*He calms down*]

Davy: A've gotta job, da. Bob Wilson set us on.

Da: Eh?

Davy: Gotta job on the quay wi' Bob Wilson.

Ma: Davy, what ye sayin'?

Davy: A'm sorry, ma.

Ma: Davy!

Da: What ye talkin' about, Bob sayed nothin' ti me.

Davy: Right enough, da. After ye'd gone 'e asked us if A wanted a start.

Ma: Ye see. Ye see what ye've done.

Da: A've told ye, woman, A know nothin' about it. [*To* **Davy**] Look, A'm yor father. Now A'm entitled ti know what's goin' on.

Davy: He's startin' four school leavers on Monday. He's got three. He asked us if a wanted the job. Twenty pounds a week.

Da: Oh, Davy, what ye done?

Davy: Twenty pounds, ma. It's ownly twelve at the Town Clerk's. It's another eight quid. [*Pause*]

Da: Well, A know nothin' about it. nothin'. [*Pause*] Anyhow, what's Bob wantin' wi four young laddies?

Davy: He's puttin' a machine in.

Da: Machine? What machine?

Davy: A filletin' machine, da.

[*There is a pause as* **Da** *struggles with the news*]

Da: A what?

Davy: A filletin' machine, da. Bob says ye just feed the fish in, it goes thro' the machine, an' comes out the other end all cut.

Da: A know what a filletin' machine is.

Davy: There's no experience necessary.

[*Pause*]

Da: Ye bugs. Nobody tells ye nothin' ti yor face.

Davy: Bob says thor installin' it this week-end. 'E reckons it'll cut fifty stone an hour.

[*Pause*]

Da: Why is it? Nobody tells ye nothin' ti yor face.

Davy: Reckons it's fantastic. Even small fish. Just rattles them thro'.

Da: S'what gets me. The' cannot come out with it.

Davy: Has these nylon gears.

Da: Fifty stone an hour eh?

Davy: That's what Bob says.

Da: Aye, well that's more'n a filleter's days work.

Davy: Bob says the blades are. . . .

Da: Oh, ti hell wi' what Bob says.

[*Pause*]

Ma: Davy! Get away out.

Davy: What's the matter, ma.

Ma: Go on, get away out.

Davy: What've A done? A mean. . . .

Ma: Just get away out, Davy. Don't bother your da.

Davy: [*Disgruntled*] A dunno! What we' always fightin' for? [*He leaves and* **Da** *slumps in a chair*]

Da: Nivvor ti yor face, that's what gets me. If they'd just come an' tell ye ti yor face.

[**Ma** *resumes her tidying up*]

Ma: Some things the' cannot say to a man's face.

Da: There was talk, like — ye know. Thor's always talk. But nobody ever comes out straight with it.

Ma: A'll pour ye out a fresh cup o' tea.

Da: No. Don't bother.

Ma: It's no bother. Look, it's still hot.

Da: No. It's all right. Look.... [*Awkward pause*] I'm sorry about the mess.

Ma: It's all right. Big seas rock the little boats. [*She pours him out a fresh cup of tea. He is hunched over and she has to go close to him to offer the tea. This is a moment of truth. Despite the abusive row, when the chips are down,* **Ma** *is the support figure*] Here!

Da: Ta! [*He takes the tea with one hand. With his other hand he reaches her.... He does not drink his tea but nurses it in his hands. The door opens and* **Alice** *enters*]

Ma: Told you ti stay out an' mind the bairn.

Alice: Met Danny Mac. Sent us up with a message for da.

Da: Message? What message?

Alice: 'E says, 'Tell yor da from Bob Wilson, not ti bother comin' down on Monday, 'cos thor's nowt expected'.

[*Pause.* **Da** *looks pathetically at* **Ma**. *He is shattered*]

Da: Ye buggar! Eh! Danny Mac! What's the matter wi' them? Bob tells Danny Mac. Danny Mac he tells her. What's the matter, the' cannot come and tell me ti me face?

Ma: Mevves be a bit hard ti tell a man to his face.... [*Regretting what she is committed to say*] that he's not wanted.

[**Da** *rouses himself to salvage his pride. He gets up from his chair and grabs his jacket*]

Da: What's 'e say? Nowt expected. Is that what 'e says. Aye, well that's what they bloody think.

[*He storms out.* **Ma** *resumes clearing up*]

Ma: Was the bairn asleep?

Alice: Yes.

Ma: Better off, stayin' with her dreams. Look, help us clear up this mess. All them papers strewed there, pick them up. There's a good lass. Stuff them back on the mantelpiece, the' might be important. [**Alice** *complies but then stops to study her school report which she discovers on the mantelpiece*] What ye readin'?

Alice: Nothin'.

Ma: Nothin'?

Alice: Jus' me school report.

Ma: Let's have a look.

Alice: What for?

Ma: Let's have a look. A want ti see it. [**Alice** *hands it over*] 'Maths – lacks con-cen-tration. English – some improvement this term. Hist'ry – capable of better. Music' – didn't knaa ye took music.

Alice: Oh' aye,

Ma: 'Music – Shows considerable, apt – apti – What's this word?

Alice: Aptitude.

Ma: Well, that's good, isn't it?

Alice: 'Spose so.

Ma: An' you've got it considerable. Well that's nice, Alice. You know it's a good thing ti be good at is music. Mevves ye should take it up. Learn the piana.

Alice: Yor jokin', ma.

Ma: No, A'm not jokin', luv. Music's a luvely thing ti hev. Somethin' A always fancied meself, learnin' the piana.

Alice: Where'd we get a piana?

Ma: Thor ownly fifty pence a week. A was thinkin' about doin' a bit part-time again. They'd have us back in the shop anytime. Yes, music, that's a good thing ti have Alice.

Alice: What would the' say round here if the' heard we had a piana?

Ma: The' wouldn't mind that. Folks likes a bit o' music. Why yor welcome anywhere if ye can play an instrument. It brings pleasure. Well, it's not just for yorself, this apt—, apti—

Alice: Aptitude.

Ma: Aye. Well that means it's like a gift. Summick ye've got inside ye. Summick that's all yor own. But ye can share it. Ye understand pet. But when ye hev summick inside ye, ye hev ti do somethin' about it. 'Cos it's always like waitin', wantin' ti be brought out into the light.

[**Alice** *does not believe anything. She switches on her radio and there is music. She picks up her comic and immerses herself in it.* **Ma** *looks helplessly at her*]

The End

Annie Kenney

Alan Pater

Cast

Annie Kenney	Frederick Pethick Lawrence
Mrs Kenney	Emmeline Pethick Lawrence
Jessie Kenney	Mary
Chatterton	Accompanist
Christabel Pankhurst	Butler
Mrs Pankhurst	**Spectators** at fairground
Sylvia Pankhurst	**Stewards** and **Spectators** at Free
Teresa Billington	Trade Hall
Charlie	**Magistrates** and **Spectators**
Chairman	in courtroom
Bell	**Prison Warder** and **Prisoners**
Halliday	**Guests** at Nelson Street
Carrick	**Committee Members**
Flora Drummond	**Tramps** on the Embankment
Mrs Roe	**Audience** at Caxton Hall
Keir Hardie	**Choir**

First televised in the 'Shoulder to Shoulder' series on BBC-2 on 10 April 1974. This is an abridged version.

Annie Kenney

Scene: **A Pennine valley**. *It is a hard, beautiful and useful landscape. As we view the valley, the hear the singing of the* **Choir**.

Choir: 'From street and square, from hill and glen,
 Of this vast world beyond my door,
 I hear the tread of marching men,
 The patient armies of the poor.

 'Not ermine-clad or clothed in state,
 Their title-deeds not yet made plain,
 But waking early, toiling late,
 The heirs of all the earth remain.'

 [*Huddled in the valley is a small town which is dominated by the spiky outlines of the cotton mill. As we look at the mill the sound of the* **Choir** *drops in volume and* **Annie Kenney's** *voice can be heard over the music*]

Choir: [*Though we will not hear the words*]
 'The peasant brain shall yet be wise,
 The untamed pulse grow calm and still;
 And blind shall see, the lowly rise,
 And work in peace Time's wondrous will.'

Annie: A big family, the Kenneys. Eleven of us. I'm the fifth.
 We live in a village in the valley.

[Beyond the mill chimneys there is a hillside on which we see a cluster of tiny figures – a long way away but they look like children]

Sunday afternoons we'd go for long walks and sometimes people thought we were a Sunday School outing, so many of us. We'd walk for miles to see the first spring flowers. Then in the evening. . . .

Scene: **The Kenney living room.** *In the light of an oil lamp,* **Mrs Kenney** *reads to her family. She is a fine, bold, working-class aristocrat: the dignity and the signs of wear-and-tear both apparent on her face. The children are in shadow.* **Annie's** *narration continues over this scene.*

Annie: . . . My mother would read to us. Somehow, the stories were always about the poor people who live in London. . . .

*[***Mrs Kenney*** *is reading the story]*

Mrs Kenney: 'The alley into which he turned might, for filth and misery, have competed with the darkest corner of this ancient sanctuary in its dirtiest and most lawless time. The houses, varying from two storeys in height to four, were stained with every indescribable hue that long exposure to the weather, damp and rottenness can impart to tenements composed originally of the roughest and coarsest materials. The windows were patched with paper, and stuffed with the foulest rags; the doors were hanging on their hinges; poles with lines on which to dry clothes, projected from every casement, and sounds of quarrelling and drunkenness issued from every room.'

[**Mrs Kenney** *continues her reading in the background as we hear* **Annie**'s *voice over*]

Annie: I think it was my mother's idea that my sister and I should join the choir. . . . It wasn't my idea, because I can't sing. . . .

[*The sound of the* **Choir** *fades in under* **Annie**'s *words and then comes in loud and hard when she stops speaking*]

Scene: **The Co-Op hall.** *A small clean, unpretentious hall in Oldham. The* **Choir** *is assembled on a stage. Behind them a large banner reads:* Oldham Clarion Vocal Union. **Annie** *and her sister,* **Jessie,** *are in the choir;* **Annie** *sings with great enthusiasm — though there might be some question about whether any sound is actually emerging.*

Choir: 'Some day, without a trumpet call,
The news will o'er the world be blown,
The heritage comes back to all;
The myriad monarchs take their own.'

[*There is a brief pause, then* **Chatterton,** *the conductor, smiles his approval*]

Chatterton: Thank you all very much, that was splendid. You've earned a short rest, while I try to remember where I put the new music. . . . [*He crosses to the piano and flips his way through a pile of untidily stacked music. In the meantime,* **Annie** *and* **Jessie** *talk*]

Jessie: Annie. . . .
Annie: Yes, love. . . .

Jessie: Are you free next Thursday evening?

Annie: I'm not sure. Mr Balfour promised to take me out to dinner at the Midland but. . . .

Jessie: Tory prime ministers always let you down, you know that. . . .

Annie: Is it something exciting?

Jessie: Jane's invited us to a special meeting of the Oldham Trades Council.

[**Annie** *is not all that impressed*]

Annie: What's special about it?

Jessie: They've got two guest speakers coming. . . .

Annie: Who?

Jessie: Teresa Billington and Christabel Pankhurst. Talking about women's suffrage. . . .

Annie: Christabel? That's Mrs Pankhurst's daughter. . . ?

Jessie: Yes.

Annie: I heard her mother speak once. . . . I didn't really understand what she was talking about. . . .

[*The opening bars of the next song for rehearsal are played on the piano*]

Chatterton: Back to work, please. We'll sing 'The Patriot's Hymn'. . . .

Annie: [to Jessie] I'll come if it isn't raining. . . .

[**Chatterton** *leads them into the song*]

Scene: **The Co-Op hall meeting.** *The same setting, but a different occasion. A group of people, including* **Annie,** *is sitting at the* *front of the audience applauding enthusiastically. On the stage,* **Christabel Pankhurst** *speaks. The small platform party includes* **Teresa Billington**.

Christabel: Now . . . we have been accused, not without reason, of being a middle-class organization pursuing middle-class aims. Let me deny the accusation here and now. This is a much bigger battle on a much larger battlefield. Consider the average middle-class lady of leisure. She is warm. She is comfortable and well fed. She has a husband to work for her, and servants to save her from soiling her hands. Tell her she is disenfranchised, she will wonder what the word means . . . and be much too polite to ask. [*Some laughter from the audience, but* **Annie** *listens hard*] Consider the working-class woman. She brings up her own children, looks after her husband, cleans the house . . . and very likely works a long shift at the mill as well. . . . Isn't this the woman who is entitled to a say in how the world . . . *her* world . . . is organized? In the words of the poet, 'We're far too low to vote the tax, But we're not too low to pay.' [*Applause*] In the past we have said to our governments: 'Are you in favour of women having the vote?' And they smile, nod their heads gravely, and agree: Yes, they are in favour . . . but unfortunately they have other, more pressing problems . . . an election to win or a war to fight . . . and women must take their turn. This year, next year, sometime, never. . . . So now we have changed the question. Now the question is: 'Will you give us the vote?' And we will demand the answer: Yes.

[**Christabel** *sits down. There is a brief pause then enthusiastic applause.* **Annie**, *staring at* **Christabel**, *joins in louder then anybody. The room fills with lively, after-the-show informal chatter as the speakers and the audience drink tea.* **Annie** *makes her way through the groups of people towards* **Christabel**.]

Annie: Miss Pankhurst. . . .

Christabel: Yes?

Annie: I just wanted to say how much I enjoyed your speech.

Christabel: I'm not so much concerned with enjoyment. Did you agree with it?

Annie: Every word.

Christabel: What can you do to help us?

Annie: Help?

Christabel: I'm not interested in people who smile, nod their heads gravely and walk away. . . .

Annie: You said that in the speech.

Christabel: We're the new kind of politicians. . . . We say the same things up there [*She indicates the platform*] . . . and down here.

[*Pause*]

Annie: I work in a mill . . . and I'm active in the trade union . . . so there's nothing to stop me organizing a meeting . . . a lot of meetings if you like . . . for the factory women, the working women.

[*There is a sense that* **Annie** *is thinking on her feet;* **Christabel** *has done her thinking long before she arrived here*]

Christabel: What's your name, dear?

Annie: Annie. Annie Kenney.

Christabel: Annie to your friends?

Annie: Yes.

Christabel: I'm Christabel to mine.

[*They shake hands: it's an affirmation, more than a token*]

Scene: **The Pankhursts' sitting-room at Nelson Street. Christabel** *is introducing* **Annie** *to the assembled Sunday afternoon company:* **Mrs Pankhurst, Teresa Billington, Sylvia Pankhurst** *and others. The introductions begin, predictably, with* **Mrs Pankhurst.**

Christabel: My mother.

Mrs Pankhurst: How lovely to meet you my dear. Christabel tells me you're going to work miracles for us on the factory floor.

Annie: [*Optimistic, as always*] I'll do my best.

Christabel: My sister, Sylvia.

Sylvia: Hello, Annie. . . .

Annie: Pleased to meet you, Miss Pankhurst.

Sylvia: [*Gently correcting*] Sylvia.

Mrs Pankhurst: Sylvia's studying in London but she's come home for the weekend to collect her secret political orders.

Christabel: Teresa Billington you met the other evening. . . .

Teresa: But everybody calls me Tess. Total lack of respect, you see.

Annie: There used to be a dog in the village called Tess.

Teresa: [*To Christabel*] I always come when I'm called . . . correct?

Christabel: Always.

[*A quiet bubble of laughter into which* **Mrs Pankhurst** *issues her next instruction*]

Mrs Pankhurst: Now you must tell us all about yourself, Annie. [*She beckons* **Annie** *to join her in a chair next to hers by the fireplace.* **Annie** *does so, and sits*]

Annie: Everything?

Mrs Pankhurst: Everything.

Annie: Can I leave out the rude bits? [*Laughter. A pause, then* **Annie** *starts her story – the words are the same as those which opened the play*] Well. . . . A big family, the Kenneys. Eleven of us. I'm the fifth.

Scene: **The Pennine valley.** *The conversation from the previous scene continues into this different setting. We see the valley and hear* **Annie's** *voice.*

Annie: We live in a village in the valley.

[**Annie** *and* **Christabel** *walk across a field overlooking the valley*]

Christabel: Is that where you work?

Annie: Where the chimneys stand, yes. I started part-time when I was ten. Full-time when I was thirteen.

Christabel: Sweated labour, as Sylvia would say.

Annie: It sometimes got a bit warm.

Christabel: So you started work in the trade union movement.

Annie: I talk too much, that's all. If the girls wanted a spokesman, they'd pick on the one that talked too much. Sensible people keep quiet and walk away. Not me. The mouth keeps flying open and the words pour out. It can be a nuisance.

[**Christabel** *laughs, delighted with* **Annie's** *company, as they walk on. They come to a dry-stone wall overlooking a breathtaking landscape and sit down*]

Christabel: Your mother sounds like a marvellous woman.

Annie: Was.

Christabel: I'm sorry. . . ?

Annie: She died at the beginning of the year. [*Pause*] I miss her a lot. We were very close. A bit like you and your mother, I think. . . . [**Christabel** *nods quiet agreement*] I miss her a lot, that's why I'd like to do something for her. A struggle, eleven of us to bring up, always a struggle. Yes, I'd like to do something.

Christabel: I liked your story about her reading to you on Sunday evenings.

Annie: Not a story. That was true. And she encouraged us to read . . . the house is full of books . . . Tom Paine, Carpenter, Blatchford, Walt Whitman. . . .

Christabel: We've got the same books. . . . [*Pause*] Every time we go walking, we must bring a notebook and pencil. Write down all the important ideas we discuss. Do you agree?

Annie: I don't have many ideas. Mostly I remember other people's. But yes . . . I agree. [*Pause*] One thing you could write down . . . if you had a notebook.

Christabel: What's that?

Annie: Dates. The dates of the meetings I'm organizing.

[**Christabel** *is delighted and surprised that* **Annie** *is moving so quickly*]

Scene: **A fairground.** *We hear a steam organ playing in the background. We are on the edge of a Wakes Week fairground. A cart is drawn up and decked with a homemade banner reading:* Votes for women. **Annie** *stands on the cart addressing the audience of about half a dozen. Other passers-by pause as they go past but for them and for most of the watchers,* **Annie** *is just another sideshow.*

Annie: I'm speaking for the women who work in the mills . . . the weavers, card-room workers, ring spinners, winders and reelers . . . working ten hours a day then going home to look after a husband, a home and a house full of children. . . . And I'm speaking for the women who work in the sweated home trades . . . fourteen hours a day for six shillings a week. *That's* the world men have made for us. *That's* the world we're going to put right when we get the vote.

[*In the crowd is an amiably boozed-up man,* **Charlie**]

Charlie: Question, missus. . . .

Annie: I'll answer any questions. . . .

[*With prospects of some fun brewing, the crowd swells to about a dozen*]

Charlie: What about horses?

Annie: What *about* horses?

Charlie: Why shouldn't horses have the vote? That horse of yours talks more sense than you do.

[*Laughter*]

Annie: Aye, and I bet he works harder than *you* do. Mind you, he doesn't drink as much. . . .

[*More laughter.* **Annie** *has obviously won this round*]

Charlie: I'll tell you this, missus . . . if I was married to you, I'd push you off Blackpool Tower.

Annie: If I was married to *you*, mister, I'd jump off Blackpool Tower.

[*She wins herself a round of applause*]

Scene: **The sitting-room at Nelson Street. Mrs Pankhurst, Christabel, Annie** *and* **Teresa Billington** *are present. The room is now more of a committee room or campaign HQ than a social setting.*

Mrs Pankhurst: I keep hearing very exciting reports of the work you're doing, Annie. . . .

Annie: I've only had one black eye so far. . . . [**Mrs Pankhurst** *is looking at a press cutting, apparently about one of* **Annie's** *meetings*] And you mustn't believe everything they put in the papers.

Mrs Pankhurst: I don't. I believe what my daughter tells me.

Teresa: What happened in Oldham?

Annie: If the choir hadn't been there, there wouldn't have been an audience at all.

Christabel: There were other people there besides the choir. . . .

Annie: Two friends of my sister's and a tabby cat that came in after a mouse. You didn't see the mouse, did you?

Teresa: A mouse? I'm glad I wasn't there.

Annie: Can be a hard life in Oldham.

Mrs Pankhurst: There'll be no mice at the Free Trade Hall.

Christabel: [*To her mother*] Except on the platform.

Annie: The Free Trade Hall? We're not having a meeting at the Free Trade Hall, are we?

Christabel: Not us. The Liberals.

Mrs Pankhurst: Winston Churchill and Sir Edward Grey . . . rousing the electorate ready for the General Election.

Annie: I shan't go to that. I've heard it all before.

Teresa: We all have.

Christabel: You're going, Annie, and so am I.

Annie: Is it compulsory?

Mrs Pankhurst: Somebody has to ask the question.

Annie: Question?

[Mrs Pankhurst *hands* Annie *a piece of paper*]

Annie: [*Reads*] 'If you are elected, will you do your best to make Woman Suffrage a Government measure?

Teresa: It's a very cunning question.

Annie: Is it?

Mrs Pankhurst: If Churchill says yes, the Government will be committed. If he says no, the Liberal women will want to know the reason why.

[Annie *looks at* Christabel]

Annie: Is it your question?

Mrs Pankhurst: Christabel's question, yes.

Annie: What if they ignore us? Or just refuse to answer?

Christabel: We have to *make* them answer.

Annie: We ask the question. And then we see what happens next . . . we might have to think fast. . . .

Christabel: That's why. . . .

Annie: [*Finishing the sentence with* Christabel] That's why *we're* going. . . .

Mrs Pankhurst: You're not frightened, are you?

Annie: If I can run meetings at pit heads and factory gates, a hall full of Liberals won't be any trouble. . . .

Mrs Pankhurst: But you must understand the real reason, Annie. . . . You know I'm a working woman, too.

Annie: I know you're the breadwinner, Mrs Pankhurst. . . .

Mrs Pankhurst: I've been threatened by my employers — if I continue to involve myself in political activities they will dismiss me. I'm happy to ignore the threat, except that I must use a little discretion. . . .

Annie: No shouting from the gallery at the Free Trade Hall.

Mrs Pankhurst: Straight to the heart of the problem, as usual.

Annie: I don't mind. I'll shout at anybody. The cause will be in good hands.

Mrs Pankhurst: I know.

Annie: Christabel, I mean. . . .

Mrs Pankhurst: Yes, the finest hands.

[*Pause*]

Annie: Christabel's not frightened of the Liberals, are you?

Christabel: No. Are you?

Annie: Me? I'm not frightened of anybody.

[*This is a simple statement of fact*]

Scene: **The Free Trade Hall.** *In the centre of the stage sits the* **Chairman** *of the meeting; in the gallery are* **Annie** *and* **Christabel**. *These central characters are surrounded by the noise of the gathering — everybody talking and nobody listening.*

Chairman: Next question, please. . . .

Annie: If you are elected, will you do your best to make Woman Suffrage a Government measure?

Chairman: May we have the next question, please . . . yes?

Christabel: You haven't answered our question.

Annie: If you are elected, will you do your best to make Woman Suffrage a Government measure?

[*There are shouts of* 'Answer the question!' *and counter-shouts of* 'Throw them out!']

Chairman: Gentleman at the back of the hall, downstairs. . . .

Annie: If you are elected, will you do your best to make Woman Suffrage a Government measure?

Chairman: May we have your question, sir? [*He gives a quiet, gentlemanly signal to the* **Stewards**] Yes, you, sir. . . .

[*Three or four* **Stewards** *come into the gallery and try to grab the girls. They struggle and unfurl their* 'Votes for Women' *banners. The noise from the hall grows as the two girls continue to shout*]

Christabel: What are you frightened of? What is the Liberal Party frightened of?

Annie: If you are elected, will you do your best to make Woman Suffrage a Government measure?

Christabel: [*To audience*] Are you prepared to see this happening in your country? In the land of the free?

Chairman: May we please have order in the hall, please! [*He bangs on the table*] Thank you, gentlemen.

[*The* **Stewards** *drag and push* **Annie** *and* **Christabel** *towards the exit doors*]

Annie: Yes or No? Will you give us the vote? Yes or No?

[*She is forced out the door to cheers and boos from the audience*]

Scene: **A magistrates court.** *Although the court is crowded and* *excited, this is a sharp contrast to the previous scene. On the magisterial bench there are five magistrates including* **Halliday**, *the chairman.* **Christabel** *and* **Annie** *are in the dock.* **Mrs Pankhurst**, **Teresa Billington** *and others seen at Nelson Street are in the public gallery.* **Carrick**, *a reporter, is among the pressmen.* **Robert Bell** *outlines the case for the prosectuion.*

Bell: Miss Kenney and Miss Pankhurst are charged with disorderly behaviour in the street and Miss Pankhurst is also charged with assaulting the police. [*Pause*] If the evidence is true, the defendants have behaved more like women from the slums. [**Annie** *is stung by this*] In spite of this, there is no desire that a heavy penalty should be inflicted, but the magistrates will be asked to take such means as to prevent a recurrence of such a scene.

[**Bell** *sits down. There is a passage of time.* **Annie** *waves to* **Teresa**; **Carrick** *works on his notes;* **Halliday** *has a mysterious whispered conversation with his colleagues.* **Christabel** *stands up to address the court*]

Christabel: In defence of my actions, I believe they were justified because of the treatment I received at the hands of Sir Edward Grey and the other speakers at the Free Trade Hall. At the time I assaulted the police officers, I was not aware that they *were* police officers. I thought they were Liberals.

[*There is laughter in the court, notably a big guffaw from* **Annie**]

Halliday: Quiet, please.

Christabel: My deepest regret is that one of the men I assaulted was not Sir Edward himself. I stand by my every action and will do so again.

[*There is a smattering of applause from the public gallery*]

Halliday: [*Breaking in*] Thank you, Miss Pankhurst.

[**Christabel** *sits down again. Again there is a passage of time.* **Teresa** and **Mrs Pankhurst** *talk*]

Teresa: I thought Christabel was absolutely splendid.

Mrs Pankhurst: Is she ever anything less?

Teresa: I suppose not. [*She looks towards* **Annie**] I wonder whether Annie. . . .

Mrs Pankhurst: Annie will also be absolutely splendid.

[**Annie** *stands up*]

Annie: I am a mill worker, a representative of the local card-room hands' association and am currently assisting in the organization of women workers for the Independent Labour Party. I went to the meeting on behalf of those women . . . as a representative of thousands of British working women, to ask certain questions of Sir Edward Grey. . . .

Halliday: We are not concerned with Sir Edward Grey.

Annie: Sir, I am very concerned with Sir Edward Grey . . . if it wasn't for Sir Edward Grey I wouldn't be standing here in this court. . . .

Halliday: Will you please limit yourself to the charges.

Annie: I'm sorry. What am I charged with? I've forgotten, with all the excitement. . . .

Halliday: Obstructing the police.

Annie: I *might* have obstructed some people and they might have been policemen. On the other hand, a lot of people obstructed me. I was hustled out of the hall. I was treated very roughly. They might have been policemen but I had no way of telling. In any case, I have no regrets about anything I did. I was acting on behalf of the working women of this country. I will do it all again, if necessary.

[**Annie** *sits down, again to a smattering of applause from the public gallery*]

Christabel: Well done.

Annie: Thank you.

Christabel: I wonder what they'll do to us?

Annie: Deportation, I should think.

Christabel: They're going away to decide. [*Pause*] But whatever it is, we're ready for them.

[*They stand along with the rest of the court as the* **Magistrates** *leave. They sit.* **Carrick** *walks past the dock and stops for a quick word*]

Carrick: Miss Pankhurst?

Christabel: Yes?

Carrick: Carrick . . . *Evening Chronicle* . . . may I have a word with you?

Christabel: On the strict understanding that you write down exactly what I say.

Annie: And we still think it's all Sir Edward Grey's fault.

[*Again we move on in time. Then* **Annie** *and* **Christabel** *stand in the dock as* **Halliday** *announces the magistrates' decision*]

Halliday: Miss Pankhurst will be fined ten shillings for assaulting the police with the alternative of seven days' imprisonment. Miss Pankhurst and Miss Kenney will be fined five shillings each for obstructing the police, with the alternative of three days' imprisonment. The sentences will be concurrent in the case of Miss Pankhurst.

Christabel: I shall pay no fine.

Halliday: Have you any goods to distrain upon?

Christabel: No. I think not.

Halliday: Miss Kenney?

Annie: I refuse to pay any fine. And I am without goods.

Halliday: You both know the alternative.

Scene: **The prison visitors' room at Strangeways.** Jessie *crosses the room and sits down to talk to* **Annie.** *There is a* **Warder** *in attendance.* **Jessie** *is more disturbed by the experience than* **Annie**]

Jessie: Annie. . . .

Annie: Hello, Jessie. . . . [*She is very cheerful*] Good of you to call in. . . .

Jessie: I've got some money to pay the fine.

Annie: I don't want anybody to pay the fine.

Jessie: That's why I thought I'd ask you first.

Annie: Good girl. [*Pause*] Spend it on a good cause, put it in the missionary box if you like.

Jessie: It said in the paper Winston Churchill wanted to pay the fines. . . .

Annie: Save the honour of the Liberal Party.

Jessie: I suppose so.

Annie: And his seat at the General Election. No, you see, Jessie . . . if we'd paid the fine . . . or if we'd gone home peacefully like they asked us . . . there'd be nothing in the papers at all. Couple of paragraphs, perhaps. But this way. . . .

Jessie: The prison way?

Annie: Yes.

Jessie: What's it really like?

[*Pause*]

Annie: It's very strange. You know it's only for three days. They tell you it's only for three days ... but you fret ... you wonder. You wonder whether they might forget what they said. That's the worst part. You feel forgotten. Will they remember at the end of three days? Will they remember to let you out? [*A pause; then* **Annie** *recovers her spirits*] But when you see the others, you realize how easy it is for you. Yesterday we all had to go to chapel. ... [*As* **Annie** *speaks we hear, quietly at first, the sound of women singing a traditional hymn; perhaps,* 'Hills of the North Rejoice'] They tell you how wicked you are and there's Hell-fire and Damnation waiting if you don't repent. But we're all just women really ... a bit sad and lost, some of them. ... [*The singing stops abruptly.* **Annie** *and* **Jessie** *sit facing each other as before*] If I had any doubts before ... about the movement ... I haven't got any now. [*Pause*] What about you, love?

Jessie: Me?

Annie: Those who are not with us ... must be. ...

Jessie: I know the rest. [*Pause*] I'm not frightened of going to prison if you're not.

Annie: You'll get your chance, my pet.

Jessie: Not pet. Sister.

[*A pause before the scene ends*]

Scene: **The prison gates.** Annie *emerges from the main door of the prison along with three other* **Women** *– all three are dressed*

drably and poorly and look much older than their years. **Annie**
*watches them until her attention is drawn by the small reception
committee awaiting her. These include* **Teresa Billington**, **Jessie
Kenney** *and* **Mrs Pankhurst** *plus at least two bouquets of flowers
and a waiting taxi. One of the other* **Women** *glances back to see
what the fuss is about before she shuffles on*]

Scene: **Nelson Street. Annie** *sits by the fire eating a hearty
breakfast off a tray. Close by is* **Carrick**, *the reporter.*

Annie: You don't mind if I eat while I'm talking to you?

Carrick: Not at all.

Annie: What did you want me to say?

Carrick: If you'd just tell us about your prison experiences,
Miss Kenney. . . .

Annie: Well. . . . [*A pause while she makes a bacon sandwich
out of the components on the tray*] We were very well treated,
I'd like to say that. No complaints about our treatment. We
had to wear prison clothing, of course. But nice warm under-
clothes . . . not pretty but warm . . . or should I not mention
that?

Carrick: Mention whatever you like.

Annie: They gave me a lovely pair of boots. One was too big
and the other was too small. And every prisoner has to have a
bath when she arrives but they thought . . . Miss Pankhurst
and myself . . . it was thought we were clean enough.

Carrick: What about the food?

Annie: The food was fine, as long as you like porridge and
brown bread. Three times on Sunday we had porridge and
brown bread. Of course, sometimes they give you brown
bread and porridge. Am I going too quickly?

Carrick: No, you're doing fine. [*He is writing all this down eagerly, because it's good copy*]

Annie: And then in church they told us not to steal, not to tell lies, not to do all sorts of things that we never do in any case, if you see what I mean. It was funny, really, but you're not allowed to laugh. [*Pause*] But no complaints. Don't forget to put that.

Carrick: I won't. [*He gets up*] Thank you very much for talking to me. . . .

Annie: That's all right. You haven't asked me if I'd be prepared to go back to prison. . . .

Carrick: I think I know the answer to that.

Annie: Good. I'm glad.

Carrick: Good morning, Miss Kenney. Enjoy your breakfast.

Annie: Thank you. You're very kind.

[**Carrick** *goes out, passing* **Teresa**, *who goes to join* **Annie**]

Teresa: You've no idea the fuss you've caused.

Annie: A good fuss or a bad fuss?

Teresa: Very good. Lots of letters from all over the country. Protest meetings. There's one at the Free Trade Hall on Saturday. Keir Hardie's going to speak.

Annie: Perhaps Sir Edward Grey will come and we'll be able to throw him out.

Teresa: 'The brave little mill girl who's won the hearts of the country. . . .'

Annie: I beg your pardon?

Teresa: That's what one of the papers said . . . one that's on our side, of course. . . .

Annie: Isn't it easy to get into the newspapers? [*This is a new discovery*] Mind you, I'm not sure I want to be a mill girl.

Teresa: It's nothing to be ashamed of.

Annie: Nobody *wants* to be a mill girl, Tess. You just get pushed into it. There's no choice.

Teresa: Isn't that what the battle is all about? Women having the choice?

[*Pause*]

Annie: I suppose it is. [*She smiles*] I don't know what I'd do if there weren't people around me, telling me what to think. [*Then, paradoxically, she becomes more serious as she poses her next question*] Is there any more bacon?

Scene: **A park. Annie** *and* **Christabel** *walk together.*

Christabel: We have a Liberal Government with a massive majority.

Annie: But Labour's won twenty-nine seats ... that helps us, doesn't it? Keir Hardie's promised to introduce a private member's bill. . . .

Christabel: He'll still need Government support ... behind the scenes.

Annie: We'll just have to carry on making a nuisance of ourselves.

Christabel: Is that enough, Annie?

[**Christabel** *takes out a notebook, opens it and makes some notes*]

Annie: What are you writing?

Christabel: We must attack the problem at its heart. It is necessary to form a London committee of the Women's Social and Political Union. A permanent London organization.

Annie: You could go to London when you finish your law studies.

Christabel: *You* could go now.

Annie: Me?

Christabel: Do you think you could rouse London to militant action?

Annie: I don't see why not. I'll need some money.

Christabel: How much? How much money to rouse London?

Annie: [*Casual, but meaning it*] Two pounds should be enough.

Scene: **Sylvia's studio.** *It is part sitting-room and, in the near future, will become part headquarters of the London committee. It has a built-in discipline, even austerity, that prevents it being a mere shambles. There are paintings on the wall and an unfinished canvas on an easel.* **Annie** *and* **Sylvia** *come in, each carrying a suitcase. They put the cases down and* **Annie** *looks at the room, eager to be impressed.*

Sylvia: [*Referring to the cases*] Is this all?

Annie: All my worldly goods.

Sylvia: A lot of people have much less.

[*Their relationship is quiet and tentative, unlike the instant chemistry that exists between* **Annie** *and* **Christabel.** *There is a knock at the door*]

Sylvia: Sit down. Make yourself at home.

Annie: Had a long sit in the train . . . I'll wander a bit if that's all right. . . . [*She wanders about, inspecting* **Sylvia's** *paintings*]

Are these all yours?

Sylvia: Yes.

Annie: They're beautiful.

Sylvia: They should be better.

Annie: No, really . . . they're lovely.

Sylvia: Thank you. [*Pause*] I don't work hard enough.

Annie: You never stop working, according to your mother.

Sylvia: I don't work hard enough at the painting. Always in trouble at the college. Give up political work, concentrate on your studies. But I take no notice.

Annie: It's the same with Christabel. [*She sits down*] She's a marvellous person, Christabel.

Sylvia: So everybody tells me.

[**Annie** *reacts quickly to* **Sylvia's** *dry comment*]

Annie: They say you're marvellous, too.

Sylvia: [*Half-smile*] And you've acquired a reputation for quick thinking. I see why.

Annie: I'm going to see Keir Hardie tomorrow.

Sylvia: There's a well-worn path from here to Keir Hardie's. . . .

Annie: I thought there might be.

Sylvia: And when you've had a day to settle in, I'll show you some of the sights. . . .

Annie: I'd like to go to the National Gallery. . . .

Sylvia: Not those sights. I mean the sights they don't talk about in polite circles . . . the East End. Have a look at some East End faces, that's the real National Gallery. . . .

[**Sylvia** *is very serious and earnest again: her true role.* **Annie's** *eyes wander again towards the paintings. She focuses on one in particular. It is an East End scene*]

Scene: **Keir Hardie's flat. Keir Hardie** *and* **Annie** *are in friendly conference: they are old friends.*

Hardie: I know you worship the ground that Christabel Pankhurst walks on . . . no doubt with good reason. But Sylvia's sowing the seeds where they'll bring forth the fruit your movement needs.

Annie: In the East End?

Hardie: Among the working classes. It'll be their support that'll win the day for you in the end.

Annie: I brought my clogs and shawl with me.

Hardie: Did you now?

Annie: I take them everywhere.

Hardie: I thought you were resolved never to wear those again.

Annie: We thought . . . if we march on Downing Street . . . or lobby Parliament, anything like that . . . the clogs and shawl look more interesting on photographs. In the newspapers. They attract attention, especially in London. That's what we think, anyway.

Hardie: That's what Christabel thinks.

Annie: It might have been her idea . . . I don't have many ideas of my own.

Hardie: Annie, my love. Just a wee warning.

Annie: What about?

Hardie: Especially now you're in London. Don't let anybody patronize you.

Annie: Who's likely to do that?

Hardie: Anybody. Believe me, Annie, I *know*. Any son or daughter of the working class who shows the brain and the intelligence to move among the Lords and Masters . . . like you . . . and like me . . . give the Lords and Masters half a chance, they'll turn you into a performing monkey. I see it in my own party. The new Labour members. They enjoy the patronage, the wining and dining . . . and it destroys them in the end. They don't even know it's happening. [*Pause*] Don't let other people pull the strings, Annie. Keep tight hold of the strings. That way, you'll keep tight hold of your own soul.

Annie: I'll do my best.

Hardie: Aye. I'll back you to survive. Now let's do some work.

Annie: That's what I'm here for.

Hardie: Have you heard of Mr and Mrs Pethick Lawrence?

Annie: I've heard a little about them.

Hardie: They're good organizers. That's the other thing you need . . . organization . . . to go with your working-class support. You'll get organization from Frederick and Emmeline . . . if you can persuade them to co-operate. . . .

Annie: I'll persuade them.

Hardie: I give you fair warning. Mrs Pankhurst tried to get them involved but they refused . . . said they were already too busy, too many commitments . . . which happens to be true. So you'll have to work a wee bit.

Annie: [*Totally confident*] It'll be all right.

Hardie: Now, if there's anything else. . . .

Annie: Yes. One thing.

Hardie: [*Anticipating her*] I know, I'll tell you which bus to catch. [*He is very warm and paternal*] Get on the first bus that comes along, mention my name to the driver and tell him where you want to go . . . you'll have no trouble.

Scene: **The Pethick Lawrence apartment. Frederick** *and* **Emmeline** *greet* **Annie.**

Butler: Miss Annie Kenney.

Frederick: [*To* **Butler**] Thank you. [*He shakes hands with* **Annie** *as the Butler goes out*] Hello, Miss Kenney.

Annie: Hello, Mr Pethick Lawrence.

Frederick: My wife, Emmeline. . . .

Emmeline: I'm delighted to meet you, Miss Kenney. . . .

Annie: I'm delighted too.

Frederick: Do sit down. [*They sit down*] Have you fully recovered from your experiences in prison?

Annie: Prison? Oh yes. I'd forgotten about prison, it was so long ago.

Frederick: Good. Now please don't think me rude, Miss Kenney, but before you tell us why you've come here . . . and we're both well enough informed to guess why you've come . . . I must ask you to be reasonably brief as we both have other meetings to attend. . . .

Annie: I want you to join our movement . . . the woman's suffrage movement.

Emmeline: What sort of help would you need?

Annie: Mr Keir Hardie suggested you'd be the ideal person to be the first National Treasurer of the Women's Social and Political Union.

[*This is rather more than* **Emmeline** *expected*]

Emmeline: The National Treasurer?

Annie: The first. He said you were efficient and business-like.

We're not efficient and business-like. They won't even answer our questions. We end up in prison.

Frederick: Have you any funds?

Annie: Not really. They gave me two pounds to come to London with, but that's nearly gone. I think we're probably in debt.

Frederick: Honorary Treasurer, with the emphasis on 'Honorary'. . . .

Annie: Part of the idea is that the Honorary Treasurer would raise funds for the campaign. It's all been Mrs Pankhurst's own money so far, and she's not a rich woman. She's as poor as me, though she doesn't admit it. Mr Keir Hardie said you'd be good at raising money.

Emmeline: What a talkative man he is.

Annie: I'm sure Sylvia would donate a painting.

Frederick: A painting?

Annie: If you decided to hold a raffle. Am I talking too much? I don't want to delay you. I mean, these are details of policy, really. . . .

Emmeline: I hope you don't want an immediate answer.

Annie: Of course not, I don't like to rush anybody. . . .

Frederick: And I'm sure Mr Keir Hardie must have said . . . give them time, let the idea simmer. . . .

Annie: Yes. He said something like that. He's a marvellous man.

Emmeline: And so eloquent.

Frederick: Very.

[*This is a private joke between them*]

Emmeline: How much time will you allow me? To simmer?

Annie: We're having a meeting tomorrow night. At Sylvia's . . . that's where I'm staying . . . 45, Park Walk, Chelsea . . . at seven-thirty. . . . If you could come along, meet Sylvia and the others . . . hear all about our campaign. . . . [*Pause*] You *will* come, won't you?

[*A pause during which* **Frederick** *and* **Emmeline** *exchange glances*]

Emmeline: No promises.

Annie: I didn't come for promises . . . just say you'll come to the meeting. . . .

Emmeline: All right.

Annie: [*She stands up*] I'll be quiet now, so you can go to your meetings. Sylvia's taking me to the East End to further my education . . . there's a lot to know, isn't there?

Frederick: Yes. Quite a lot.

Annie: But it's all exciting.

Scene: **Sylvia's studio.** *The room is set for a committee meeting. Around the table are eight people:* **Sylvia, Annie, Emmeline Pethick Lawrence, Mrs Roe,** *the landlady, plus* **Mrs Clarke, Mary Neal, Mrs Fenwick Miller** *and* **Mrs Martell:** *none of these last four speaks during the scene.* **Sylvia** *is acting as chairman of the meeting.*

Sylvia: The resolution is that the Central London Committee of the Women's Social and Political Union be formed. . . . [*She looks for a show of hands: all hands go up*] Unanimously. [*She notes this in the minutes – she's acting as secretary, too*] Next. The post of Honorary Secretary.

Annie: I propose Sylvia.

Mrs Roe: Seconded.

Sylvia: Are there any other nominations?

[*There are none*]

Annie: I think you'd better write 'Unanimously'.

[**Sylvia** *looks at them: all hands go up*]

Sylvia: Thank you all very much. I'll do my best. [*There is a pause while she makes the note in the minutes*] Next. The position of National Treasurer.

Annie: I propose Mrs Pethick Lawrence.

Mrs Roe: Seconded.

Emmeline: Perhaps Mrs Pethick Lawrence isn't prepared to accept the nomination. . . .

Sylvia: If there are any questions we can answer to help make up your mind. . . .

Emmeline: Well, I know you have no money.

Sylvia: Correct.

Emmeline: Do you have any place in mind as an office? A headquarters?

Sylvia: We thought here. . . .

Mrs Roe: You're all most welcome.

Emmeline: What about your studies?

Sylvia: I'll. . . .

Mrs Roe: [*Breaking in*] She'll do that through the night, same as she does at the moment. . . .

Emmeline: What about the rest of the London organization?

Sylvia: We *are* the London organization.

Emmeline: I see. [**Pause**] Any . . . assets? Stationery? Stamps? A typewriter?

Annie: [*Sudden thought*] Flora Drummond might get us a typewriter. She works for the Oliver company in Manchester. . . .

Sylvia: But I think you'll be starting with a totally clean sheet, Mrs Pethick Lawrence. [*She smiles.* **Emmeline** *hesitates*]

Emmeline: I'll accept the nomination.

Annie: I think it will be carried unanimously.

Emmeline: I shouldn't be surprised.

[*It is unanimous*]

[*Interval, if wanted*]

Scene: **Sylvia's studio. Sylvia** *and* **Annie**, *alone after their meeting, are drinking their late-night cocoa.*

Annie: I did enjoy this evening.

Sylvia: The meeting.

Annie: Yes. I really think we're getting somewhere. You know ... if anybody told me ... a year ago ... the way things were going to happen ... being in London, meeting people like the Pethick Lawrences. . . .

Sylvia: People like the Pethick Lawrences?

Annie: Yes. . . . [*She is puzzled by the challenge in* **Sylvia's** *voice*] They are rather special, aren't they?

Sylvia: They've got money *and* a social conscience. It's an unusual combination.

Annie: It's not *their* fault they've got money. . . .

Sylvia: No. It's ours. Your fault and my fault.

Annie: I'm sorry, I . . . don't understand.

Sylvia: [*Breaking in*] Annie. You're happier than you were a year ago. You find fulfilment in the work.

Annie: Of course.

Sylvia: But you mustn't make the mistake of thinking it's for your benefit. I'm not important and you're not important. It's the mistake that Christabel makes.

Annie: Christabel?

Sylvia: The lovely lady Christabel. She's fighting for the emancipation of women . . . but the person she's really emancipating is herself. Watch her when she's making a speech . . . or watch her when she comes out of prison . . . you're watching an emancipated woman. . . . [*Pause*] But that's not the problem.

Annie: Tell me.

Sylvia: Watch the prison gates. When one of our people is released.

Scene: **The prison gates.** *Exactly as before, when the reception committee met* **Annie. Teresa Billington, Jessie Kenney** *and* **Mrs Pankhurst** *stand outside the gates. There are at least two bouquets of flowers and a waiting taxi. One of the other released women glances back to see what the fuss is about before she shuffles on. Against these images, we hear* **Sylvia's** *voice.*

Sylvia: You see a reception committee . . . flowers . . . kisses and applause and smiles for the world. A taxi to take you to a hearty breakfast and an interview with the press. But watch the other women. The ones who slink away silently . . . no flowers, no kisses, no taxis, probably no breakfast either . . . they're the ones, Annie. . . .

Scene: **Sylvia's studio.** *This is a continuation of the earlier scene.* **Annie** *and* **Sylvia** *are as they were.*

Sylvia: The battle's for those women . . . not for us . . . we don't matter.

[*Pause*]

Annie: Like . . . the women on the Thames Embankment?
Sylvia: Yes.

Scene: **The Thames Embankment.** *A group of men and women is sleeping rough on the Embankment. One of the women is by any outward physical and social standards a tramp; it is difficult to be precise about her age because she's really timeless and universal. If she had a name, she lost it: we will call her* **Mary.** **Mary** *smiles at* **Annie:** *the teeth are irregular but the spirit is shining.*

Annie: Would you like a cup of tea?

Scene: **A caff.** *'Caff' is an exact description of this establishment.* **Annie** *and* **Mary** *sit at a rough wooden table with large mugs of tea.*

Mary: You're very kind, dear.
Annie: Not really.

Mary: They sometimes do this, you know, The well-dressed ladies . . . ladies of quality . . . they come down the Embankment and give us food or something to drink or new boots. . . . We watch for them coming . . . try to look cold and hungry as they walk past so's they'll notice us. . . . Oh, yes, ladies of quality, very refined. . . . [*Pause*] Not like you.

Annie: I do my best.

Mary: Oh, you've got quality, dear. But not born to it.

Annie: I used to be a mill girl.

Mary: From the North?

Annie: Yes.

Mary: I can tell. I've travelled a great deal, you see. Oh yes, you're one of us. You know what it's like . . . being shut in.

Annie: Shut in? Yes, I know about that. I've been in prison.

Mary: Prison? So you'll know about freedom as well.

Annie: I've walked the Pennine hills. . . .

Mary: Cathedrals I like.

Annie: Did you say cathedrals?

Mary: Surprises people, that. I've seen them all, well, mostly. Salisbury and Durham and Truro. . . .

Annie: Walking?

Mary: No money for fares. I take my own time. There's no hurry when you're a pilgrim. You know where you're going. You know it'll be there when you get there.

Annie: Like the great city.

Mary: That I couldn't say. I've always wanted to go to Russia. Now *there's* a pilgrimage for you. But I don't suppose I'll ever go. I stick to my cathedrals. They're always there. Twice as big as you expected. Twice as grand. They don't let you down.

[*Pause*]

Annie: Do you believe in God?

Mary: Not a lot, dear, to be honest. Don't be offended but. . . .

Annie: I'm not.

Mary: When you're lying there and you're cold and you're hungry, well, if you start believing in God you're bound to say he's not making a very good job of things. I might start believing in him when he makes a better job of running things. [*Pause*] No. I believe in my cathedrals, I believe in them, oh yes. [*Pause*] Always there, right where you expected them.

Scene: **Sylvia's studio.** *In effect this is a continuation of* **Annie's** *and* **Sylvia's** *conversation after the meeting.*

Sylvia: For Christabel, the movement is her life.

Annie: And your mother too?

Sylvia: Her life as well. But that's not enough. For me, it has to be a sacrifice of my life.

Annie: You're not like Christabel or your mother, are you?

Sylvia: Different . . . but the same. Different ways of doing things. . . but the same passion. When I quarrel with my mother . . . you've never heard us quarrel have you? You can hear it for miles around . . . but we quarrel because we share the same passions . . . because we care. . . .

Annie: But I don't understand the difference. . . .

Sylvia: Simple. My mother . . . and Christabel too. They devote their life to the movement . . . they haven't sacrificed anything else. I have. If I was sent on this earth to do anything, it was to paint pictures. I may not be very good at it, you can't tell . . . but it's a hard job being a bad artist even.

... It's what I really want to do, Annie, paint pictures. But when I look at the women on the embankment ... painting pictures seems like an obscenity. Just ... not important. ... Only to me is it important. And that's not good enough.

Scene: **Keir Hardie's flat. Hardie** *sits reading through his papers. There is a sharp, business-like knock on the door.*

Hardie: Come in.

[**Annie** *comes in very briskly. The whole sequence should be busy and practical: a sharp contrast to the preceding scene*]

Annie: Good morning.

Hardie: Good morning, Annie. You're looking very pleased with yourself. ...

Annie: We've done it!

Hardie: What have you done?

Annie: We've booked the Caxton Hall for our first public meeting in London. February sixteenth. The day the new Liberal Government assembles ... but it's *us* they'll be listening to. ...

Hardie: The Caxton Hall? It's a big hall, it'll take some filling. ...

Annie: We'll fill it.

Hardie: As long as it's with people, not with hot air. ...

Annie: All Sylvia's working women from the East End, they'll be coming. ...

Hardie: Have you asked them?

Annie: Not yet.

Hardie: Somebody will have to pay their fares to get them there. . . .

Annie: And we'll give them something to eat and drink when they arrive at the hall. . . .

Hardie: Good girl, you're thinking ahead of me. . . .

Annie: Except that what with that, and the hire of the hall, and cost of printing and. . . .

Hardie: You're short of money.

Annie: That's why I came to see you.

Hardie: I was thinking it was pure and simple affection. . . .

Annie: Well, of course it's that as well but . . . we really need another fifty pounds. The Pethick Lawrences have helped but we're still short. . . .

Hardie: Are you looking for a loan or a gift?

Annie: Honestly, we're not fussy . . . we're fully prepared to accept either. . . .

Hardie: The nobility shines like a beacon. . . .

Annie: I beg your pardon?

[*Pause*]

Hardie: There's W. T. Stead . . . he might be prepared to help . . . and Isabel Ford. . . . Mind you, I've got about a dozen schemes of my own that I'm trying to enlist their support for. . . .

Annie: If you just give me their addresses. . . . [*Hesitates*]

Hardie: Yes?

Annie: I'll race you to them.

Hardie: I wouldn't even enter a race against you, Annie Kenney. . . .

Scene: **Sylvia's studio.** *The door flies open and Annie comes in, very pleased with herself.*

Annie: I got the money! [*She pauses and does a kind of double take. In the room, apart from* **Sylvia,** *are* **Teresa Billington** *and* **Jessie Kenney**] Jessie! Tess!

Teresa: We thought you might need a little help. . . .

Annie: Oh, we do . . . no question, we need some help. . . .

[*She crosses to them and they embrace* **Annie** *in turn*]

Jessie: How are you, Annie?

Annie: I'm fine.

Jessie: You look exhausted, but you always did.

Annie: [*To Teresa*] How long are you staying in London?

Teresa: Permanently, I hope.

Annie: That's marvellous.

Sylvia: How much money did you get, Annie?

Annie: Two twenty-five-pound loans . . . but they might turn into very long-term loans. . . . Do you think we might buy a typewriter? [*She turns to* **Jessie**] We want to circulate every Member of Parliament.

[*All this time* **Sylvia** *is quietly sketching on a drawing pad.* **Annie** *crosses to her to have a look*]

Annie: That's lovely, Sylvia. . . . [*To the others*] Sylvia's designing our banner for the meeting. . . . [*To Sylvia*] Did you get any chalks?

Sylvia: On the table.

[*On the table is a box of chalks.* **Annie** *picks up the box*]

Sylvia: Courtesy of the art college.

Scene: **A street.** *It is in a working-class neighbourhood of the East End.* **Annie** *is on her hands and knees chalking on the pavement. It is tedious and uncomfortable work. She writes:* 'WSPU Public Meeting. Caxton Hall. Main Speaker: Mrs Pankhurst. Votes for Women!' *She adds artistic touches – multi-coloured underlinings, shadowing the letters and so on. She rubs her knees as she stands up to inspect her work.*

Scene: **Keir Hardie's flat. Hardie** *and* **Sylvia** *are talking.*

Sylvia: So we wondered whether we might have the occasional use of this place for the next few days. . . .

Hardie: As long as you don't expect me to prepare meals for you.

Sylvia: We might even prepare an occasional meal for you. . . .

Hardie: That's very gracious, Sylvia, I accept your offer.

Sylvia: A token of our admiration and affection. . . .

Hardie: And what's the ulterior motive?

Sylvia: You've got a telephone. We haven't.

[*They smile, because it's the easy teasing of old comrades*]

Scene: **Sylvia's studio. Annie** *and* **Teresa** *are in the foreground – * **Annie** *still with her street-chalking working clothes on.*

Annie: How many loaves will we need?

Teresa: How many women are coming?

Annie: We won't really know until the night. . . .

Teresa: You'd better order five loaves and two fishes. . . .

Jessie: And leave the rest to Mrs Pankhurst. . . .

Flora: The Gospel according to St Matthew says it was seven loaves.

Annie: I'm going to order one hundred.

Teresa: Can we afford it?

Annie: I'll open an account somewhere. I've learned *that* much about London.

Scene: **Keir Hardie's flat. Sylvia** *is alone: on the telephone.*

Sylvia: Hello? Is that *The Times?* I'd like to speak to the editor please. . . . [*She waits, then speaks as the* **Editor** *materializes at the other end*] Good afternoon, this is Sylvia Pankhurst of the Women's Social and Political Union. Did you receive our letter about the Caxton Hall meeting?

Scene: **An East End street. Annie** *is struggling with a huge poster advertising a meeting. She is attempting to stick it to a bare brick wall.*

Scene: **Sylvia's studio.** *In contrast to the last time we were here, this is a quiet, wee-small-hours scene.* **Annie** *is asleep in a* *chair by the fire.* **Sylvia** *is painting a banner – which she has fixed so that it covers most of one wall of the studio.* **Teresa** *comes in with a tray carrying three cups of cocoa.*

Teresa: She's asleep.

Sylvia: Yes. [*Pause*] She was chattering away, sixteen to the dozen, then suddenly it stopped.

Teresa: I won't wake her. [*She puts the tray down and takes a drink to Sylvia*] There.

Sylvia: Thank you, Tess.

Teresa: Do you know what time it is?

Sylvia: No.

Teresa: Twenty past two.

Sylvia: I always work well after midnight. As my ladies would say . . . [*She goes into a Cockney accent*] focuses the mind somefink remarkable.

Teresa: Yes, but. . . . [*She hesitates*] You could do yourself permanent damage.

Sylvia: I've already done that. So it's no longer a problem.

Scene: **Keir Hardie's flat.** *Now it's* **Annie** *on the telephone.*

Annie: Yes . . . one hundred loaves to be delivered to the Caxton Hall tomorrow night . . . by five o'clock? That's very good. . . . [*The caller at the other end of the phone is about to hang up but* **Annie** *calls him back*] There's just one more thing. . . . You don't happen to know where we can borrow a tea urn . . . well, not one, more like a dozen, I suppose. . . . Thank you, we've already tried the Salvation Army. . . .

Scene: **Sylvia's studio.** *The banner is about to be 'unveiled': of course* **Sylvia** *would not dream of such a theatrical gesture as a physical unveiling. She just stands aside.*

Sylvia: I'll have to call that finished.

[**Annie**, **Jessie** *and* **Teresa** *all stop whatever they doing to look*]

Sylvia: I've had to rush it too much, but. . . .

Annie: If you want a job doing, you ask a busy person. . . .

Jessie: What our mother always said.

Teresa: She was right. It's absolutely splendid.

[*They are standing in a group admiring* **Sylvia's** *work – and by implication their own – when the door opens and* **Mrs Pankhurst** *walks in*]

Mrs Pankhurst: So this is the mad-house. . . .

Sylvia: I beg your pardon, mother?

Mrs Pankhurst: The lunatic asylum.

Sylvia: What are you talking about?

Mrs Pankhurst: I'm talking about sensible, grown women who are sent to London to organize political action and in a matter of two or three weeks you book the largest hall you can get your hands on, heaven knows at what cost to the movement . . . and I find myself committed to addressing a meeting that will be attended by rows and rows of empty seats. Is it too late to cancel it?

Sylvia: Much too late, yes.

Mrs Pankhurst: It will set back the cause several years. Just imagine what the press will say . . . last night Mrs Pankhurst addressed a meeting in London . . . the first London rally of the Women's Social and Political Union . . . she received a lukewarm reception from an audience of twenty-five, most of them friends of the family . . .

Sylvia: That's not fair.

Mrs Pankhurst: I was making speeches before you were born. You develop instincts for these things. . . .

[There is a rather uneasy silence. **Annie** *leaps in]*

Annie: You're wrong, Mrs Pankhurst. The hall will be full. Packed to overflowing.

Mrs Pankhurst: Who will this splendid audience consist of?

Annie: Our supporters from the East End.

Mrs Pankhurst: How many? Ten? Twenty?

Annie: We think about four hundred. We're paying their fares and we're feeding them when they arrive at the hall.

Mrs Pankhurst: If this were Oldham or Manchester, I would believe you. As it is, I can only hope and pray that you are right. *[She goes to the door]* I'll see what I can do to rescue the movement from this disaster.

[She sweeps out. There is another uneasy silence. **Sylvia** *looks across at* **Annie**]

Sylvia: Thank you.

Annie: I hope I wasn't rude.

Sylvia: It's very hard to insult my mother. It might do her good if more people tried. . . .

Annie: *[Crossing over to* **Sylvia**] It's a lovely banner.

Sylvia: Good. [*Pause*] Annie. I *do* hope you're right.

Annie: [*Revealing for the first time* her *secret fears about the meeting*] Sylvia. So do I.

Scene: **Caxton Hall.** *The rows of empty seats suggest at first that the worst fears have been realized. Then, at the back of the hall, we find a group, including* **Annie,** **Jessie** *and* **Teresa,** *working at a trestle table preparing food.* **Annie** *is hard at work slicing bread while* **Jessie** *and* **Teresa** *are buttering.*

Annie: Do you think I ordered too much? [*She pauses between loaves to exercise her aching wrists*]

Jessie: All we can do is wait and see.

Teresa: Say a quick prayer. That might help.

Annie: I was sure everything would be all right until Mrs Pankhurst. . . . [*She is interrupted by a shout from* **Sylvia** *off stage*]

Sylvia: Is that all right? [*She comes onto the stage and arranges a banner behind the table which is set for the platform party. She has made a good and colourful job of the platform*]

Teresa: [*Shouts*] It looks marvellous.

Jessie: [*Quietly*] I hope somebody's here to see it.

Teresa: I'm waiting to hear Mrs Pankhurst apologize.

Annie: Whatever for?

Jessie: You know what for.

Teresa: She had no right to say those things to you and Sylvia. . . .

Annie: Whether there's five people or five hundred, all Mrs Pankhurst has to do is make a speech. That's all. Nothing more. [**Annie** *doesn't bear grudges*]

Teresa: You've got to make a speech, too, don't forget.

Annie: I prefer cutting bread. [**Teresa** *pushes another loaf towards* **Annie**]

Teresa: Thank you. [*As* **Annie** *cuts another loaf she quietly practises her speech*]

Annie: 'Madam Chairman, ladies, sisters . . . this is the first public meeting to be held in London. . . .' [**Sylvia** *enters*]

Sylvia: Annie, you've won! [*She opens the doors and* **Women** *enter in a mass.* **Annie** *sighs a deep sigh of relief and closes her eyes briefly.* **Annie** *mounts the stage to make her speech. The audience is mainly composed of working-class women with a sprinkling of middle-class ladies wearing, in some case, their servants' clothes in a vain effort not to look conspicuous. The East End contingent has red Labour Party banners but these are furled up and concealed at this point. On the platform we see all our principals:* **Mrs Pankhurst, Sylvia, Christabel, Teresa, Emmeline, Jessie** *and behind them, the banner*]

Annie: Madam Chairman, ladies . . . sisters. . . . This is the first public meeting to be held in London by the Women's Social and Political Union. That may sound to you like a lot of big words . . . and so they are to me, because I had to practise that bit several times before the meeting to be sure of getting it right. [*Ripple of laughter*] I won't use any more big words. I'll leave that to those who are cleverer than me . . . which means practically everybody. I'm just going to tell you what this movement means to me. It all started, believe it or not, because I sang in a choir . . . which is very silly because I can't even sing. [*Laughter*] I used to open my mouth in time with the others, and hope that nobody would notice there was no noise. It was through the choir that I met the Pankhursts . . . and through them my life changed. When I try to explain how my life has changed, I keep thinking of one of the songs we used to sing. I won't sing it now but I will tell you some of the words. . . . like this it goes. . . .

'From street and square, from hill and glen,
Of this vast world beyond my door,
I hear the tread of marching men,
The patient armies of the poor.

'Not ermine-clad or clothed in state,
Their title-deeds not yet made plain,
But waking early, toiling late,
The heirs of all the earth remain.'

And it finishes. . . .

'Some day, without a trumpet call,
The news will o'er the world be blown,
The heritage comes back to all;
The myriad monarchs take their own.'

I am one of the patient armies of the poor. And so are most
of you. But we're not content to be patient any longer.
[*There are cries of:* 'Hear. Hear.'] It is time to take back our
heritage. It is time to take back our own. I believe . . . we
believe . . . that the first step must be the vote. We all know
the ancient cry: No taxation without representation. I think
it's time to alter that. We should say: no exploitation without
representation. No slums without representation. No oppres-
sion, no starvation, no degredation without representation. . . .
And when the day comes that we – the women of Great
Britain – have representation . . . I predict that in a strange
and miraculous way, we will look and we will see that these
other things have vanished . . . the exploitation and the slums
and the starvation. . . . At the very least, we can't make a
worse mess than our gentlemen politicians . . . and at the
very best, we shall walk equally with men, and with them take
possession of our true heritage. [*Applause*] My sisters . . . I
thank you for listening to me. Now it is my great honour and
privilege to introduce our very special guest speaker . . . beloved of all Prime Ministers . . . beloved of all of us here in
this hall: Mrs Pankhurst. . . .

[**Mrs Pankhurst** *stands up and crosses to* **Annie**. *There is loud and enthusiastic applause for both of them.* **Annie** *is about to return to her seat but* **Mrs Pankhurst** *takes her hand and forces her to acknowledge the applause*]

Mrs Pankhurst: Annie. . . . I apologize.

Annie: There's nothing to apologize for. . . .

Mrs Pankhurst: Oh me of little faith.

Annie: Listen. . . .

[*They turn again towards the audience.* **The Women** *are standing, Labour Party banners are displayed and we hear, without identifying the singer, a* **Woman** *singing the opening lines of* The Red Flag. *The singing swells to a mighty chorus. The platform party join in and the audience sway their banners*]

All: 'The workers' flag is deepest red,
It shrouded oft our martyred dead.
And ere their limbs grew stiff and cold
Their life-blood dyed its every fold.
Then raise the scarlet banner high,
Beneath its folds we'll live and die.
Though cowards flinch and traitors sneer,
We'll keep the red flag flying here.'

[*As the song ends the applause and cheering builds and then dies away in a sudden long echo. The hall is now deserted and* **Annie** *sits alone.* **Sylvia** *and* **Flora** *come on to the platform and start removing the decorations. Their voices murmur.* **Teresa** *walks past* **Annie**]

Teresa: Look. [**Annie** *looks.* **Teresa** *holds up a five-pound note to show her*] Five pounds. Donation from Lady Carlisle.

Annie: Good.

Teresa: That's nearly fifty pounds in donations and promises. . . .

Annie: Good.

[**Teresa** *walks on to tell somebody else the good news.* **Mrs Pankhurst** *is with a group of* **Women** *across the hall.* **Annie's** *eyes move briefly in her direction*]

Mrs Pankhurst: We're lobbying Parliament tomorrow . . . and there's a very good chance Campbell Bannerman will receive a deputation in the very near future. . . .

[**Mrs Pankhurst's** *voice fades as* **Christabel** *approaches* **Annie.** *She sits down in a seat near* **Annie**]

Christabel: Tired?

Annie: Five minutes . . . to get my breath back.

Christabel: Don't worry. It really happened.

Annie: My mother used to say: You don't know your own strength until you try.

Christabel: Even got money to pay some of the bills.

[*Pause.* **Christabel** *takes out her notebook*]

Annie: Still the notebook?

Christabel: There's more to write down. More every day.

Annie: Yes.

Christabel: It says here . . . London.

Annie: Well done, Christabel. This *is* London.

Christabel: In the summer . . . when I finish my law studies . . . mother's going to sell up in Manchester. We're moving down here.

Annie: The heart of the Empire.

Christabel: Our Empire. [*Pause*] And it says here . . . 'Singing'. . . . [*She refers to her notebook*]

Annie: Funny thing to write down.

Christabel: You said in your speech tonight . . . you can't sing.

Annie: I can't.

Christabel: You can sing, Annie. Tonight you did.
[*Pause*]

Annie: Well . . . I thought, once or twice, just the odd sentence in the speech . . . I thought it was me talking and not somebody else. That makes a change.

Christabel: You sang. [*Pause*] Lobbying Parliament tomorrow.

Annie: Yes. [*Brief pause*] Tonight the song. Tomorrow . . . Westminster. The day after . . . the great city. [*She looks at her hands*] Look all chalk and breadcrumbs.

[*They are the last two in the hall. Slowly they make their way out.* **Annie** *pausing here and there to pick up a discarded poster or such. We hear the* **Choir** *singing over their departure*]

Choir: 'Some day, without a trumpet call,
The news will o'er the world be blown,
The heritage comes back to all;
The myriad monarchs take their own.'

[*The music fades. Somebody switches the lights out. Darkness*]

The End

Here Comes the Sun

Barrie Keeffe

Characters

The girls	*The boys*
Lynne	**Tony**
Karen	**Al**
Ali	**Sid**
Helen	**Steve**
Paula	**Andy**, a photographer
Janet	

Staff of the hotel and holiday company
Peter, a courier
Alberto, a waiter
Waiters (five)
Guardia (two)
Alfredo, a Flamenco dancer
Rick, an Englishman working as a barman in Spain
Rod, an English member of a pop group, living in Spain
Kitty, a German holidaymaker
Other **Holidaymakers**, **Hotel Workers**, etc.

Commissioned and first performed by the National Youth Theatre at the Jeanetta Cochrane Theatre, London, on 16 August 1976. The music indicated is that used in the original production. The music may be changed — the more up to date the better.

Here Comes the Sun

Act 1

Scene: **The patio outside a package holiday hotel in Spain.**
Chairs and tables with beach umbrellas are scattered around the
patio. The hotel and its entrance doors are set upstage right, and
Rick's Bar is offstage right. The hotel swimming pool is offstage
left; we see the foliage fencing it. Before the scene begins a
medley of numbers, ending with the Beatles' Here Comes the Sun,
is heard. It plays on into the lights for the scene and fades when
the **Girls** *enter. It is night. The patio is deserted. There is the*
sound of a coach stopping off, voices, then the coach driving
off again. **Ali, Lynne, Helen** *and* **Karen** *enter. The music fades as*
they look around and pace about.

Ali: It's . . . it's beautiful.

Lynne: Yeah.

Ali: Just as I imagined.

Lynne: Better than the brochure?

Helen: That was only an artist's impression.

Lynne: That's what I mean. When you see an artist's impression
you expect the worst. Artist's impression of a Benidorm hotel
— you expect it to actually look like the ape house at Man-

chester Zoo. That's what I thought last year. This looks like it's supposed to look. Good omen.

[*Pause*]

Ali: Really great, eh, Helen?

Helen: Me ears are still buzzing. I can't get them to pop.

Lynne: Make out you're swallowing a ping pong ball. That'll clear them.

Helen: I can't hear anything except – sounds like the Niagra Falls are practising in me head. The right one's not working at all.

Karen: I fancy a drink.

Ali: Don't ask Helen. She's got one ear.

[*They laugh exaggeratedly with nerves and tiredness. There is a pause as they pace about. Ali tries various chairs. Karen looks over flowerbeds at the pool*]

Lynne: That smell. I remember that smell, from last year.

Ali: It's a fabulous smell.

Lynne: You remember smells better than other things.

Ali: I wish Hull smelt like this. It's just how you said it'd be, Lynne. All so exotic. I felt it as soon as we got off the plane. I thought: Stuff Cornwall, son. Never again.

Lynne: And still so hot.

Ali: The shadows we're making, so vivid . . . the air, so bright.

Lynne: Three o'clock in the morning. And I'm sweating. Me dad'll be getting up for the market in half an hour. . . . Poor sod. Hey, what's up, Helen?

Helen: Imagining I'm swallowing a ping pong ball and – it's got stuck.

Ali: We'll go back home as brown as berries.

Lynne: Last year I went home *black*. And I was only here for ten days. Two whole weeks this time. I can't imagine how dark I'll go home.

Karen: You can't get darker than black, Lynne.

Lynne: I was jet black last year. I saw me dad in the market on the way back from the station. He looked right through me. I said, 'Dad, it's me'. He said: 'My gawd, Lynne, I thought you was a jungle bunny.' [*They laugh*] I wore nought but pastel shades and no tights for weeks. And white knickers. In the pub I'd cross me legs very nonchantly, allowing the geezers a showing of deep tanned thigh, showing it off against me white pants. God, I looked so fantastic I could have fancied meself.

Ali: [*Staring out across the pool*] Isn't it fantastic, that view. Right across the bay, all them lights.

Lynne: That's Tossa.

Ali: Just that name . . . the names are so fantastic. Compared to home. Tossa . . . Benidorm . . . Madrid . . . España . . . Salami.
. . .

Lynne: Barcelona . . . El   Cordobés . . . Sitges . . . Lloret   de Mar. . . .

Ali: Compared to — Hull.

Karen: Coronation Street . . . Hull Kingston Rovers. . . .

Lynne: Sardine Alley. . . . The Coalhouse. . . .

Ali: And . . . like those stewards . . . jabber jabber jabber, señorita. Instead of —

Lynne: 'Give us a fag, darlin'.' Oh, it's so different here, it's a different world. And everything here goes on all night. And up there, see, up there —

Ali: Look, Karen, up there.

Karen: Where?

Helen: Up there, oh yeah, up there.

Lynne: Well, up there in them hills – in the pine forests there's this clearing they've cleared, and made an open air night club. Oh it's great. We go on the second Tuesday. And it's all included.

Ali: Fantastic.

Helen: How long do we have to wait here, Lynne?

[*Slight pause. They are all a bit anxious*]

Lynne: Well.... [*Pause*] Not long. See, the other coach follows with our baggage. The first coach deposits the people and the second coach follows and deposits the baggage. Then, when we've got our baggage we can check in.

Ali: I'm starving.

Lynne: So am I.

Karen: And thirsty.

Lynne: Liberty, the price of them drinks on the plane. I tell you the drink here – *sangría.*

Helen: I remember you asking for that in the King's Head at home.

Lynne: I remember what the barman said, and all. I can feel the chains unwinding from me.... I'm being overwhelmed with ... freedom!

Karen: This is ridiculous. Where's the Manager, where's the hotel staff, where's the courier – *Where's the bloody baggage?*

Lynne: It'll be here any minute.

Karen: But shouldn't there at least be a porter to check us in?

Lynne: They work such long hours. They only have three hours' sleep a night for seven months.

Ali: I expect that's why Spaniards are so slim.

Karen: I'll have a look in reception. [*She goes off shouting*]

Wakey, wakey, rise and shine. [*She exits*]

Lynne: Right mistake asking her to come, moody bitch.

Helen: I could sleep for a week.

Lynne: I'll wake you up at nine. No, really – get up early and sleep all day by the pool. Or on the beach. Get a golden tan, like a toothpaste commercial, and then – wide awake for the night's. . . .

[*Enter* **Karen**]

Karen: The reception is deserted. Can't we just nick the keys and go to bed? Where is that courier, the great tart? And where is our baggage? If someone doesn't turn up – if something doesn't happen in the next five minutes . . . I'll smash something. [*There is a pause as she looks about for something to smash. Then she makes a megaphone with her hands and hollers*] Hello, anyone there? [*Pause*] Real Madrid are a load of rubbish. [*Pause*] I was Franco's mistress. [*Pause*] King Carlos is a pouftenberger.

[**Peter**, *the courier, enters – exhausted and out of breath*]

Pete: I expect you've been wondering what had become of me.

Karen: Our courier has extra-sensory perception.

Pete: I thought Anita was going to check you in.

Helen: Anita?

Karen: The big blonde tart at the airport?

Pete: Aye, that's her. She's supposed to be your courier.

[**Rick** *enters. He is rather drunk*]

Rick: You won't see much of her, Pete, I tell you. Her sodding Harringay speedway rider flopped in this afternoon. Bought her a mink coat.

Pete: Charming.

Ali: Are you all right?

Rick: I've just run up the hill. It's a very steep hill.

Pete: One of the steepest hills I've seen.

Rick: I used to be able to run up that hill in seven and a half
minutes. [*They look curiously at him*] And then, one day,
it came to me: What's the bloody point? I'm not much into
all that philosophical crap – but I couldn't get it out of me
head. There was no point. Makes you think, don't it?

[*Pause*]

Helen: It certainly does.

Rick: [*To* **Karen**] I used to see you at the Playboy Club.
You look different without the pointed ears and the fluff up
your backside.

Karen: You've never seen me there.

Rick: That's funny. Have a nice holiday. [*He leaves the group
and retires to a table where he sits*]

Helen: How peculiar.

Karen: Who was he?

Pete: That's Rick. He's got the bar down there – the Howling
Budgie.

Karen: Odd name.

Pete: He's a very odd sort of bloke. Oh, the authorities were
furious when they discovered the name. Thought he was taking
the mick.

Karen: I expect he was. Who is he?

Pete: Another Englishman running away from something and
hoping instead he'll make a fast buck on the candyfloss
world of the Costa Brava. Oh dear, what a day.

Ali: I'm sorry about that, but where's the baggage?

Pete: Look I'm just a red brick second-class honours in languages, love, I'm not sodding Superman.

Karen: At the airport, you told us to leave our baggage –

Pete: Look I'll sort it all out. You lot check in – [*Shouts at door of hotel*] José, José Blabber blabber blabber. [*To girls*] Everything'll be all right. Just go through there to José. Show him your passports and folder and he'll get you to your rooms – something to eat and drink. Follow me. Your luggage will be here in a trice.

[*They all go, except* **Karen**. *She is about to follow when she realizes that* **Rick** *is still there, slumped with a glass at the table*]

Karen: He's not very well organized, is he?

Rick: What do you expect for a hundred quid including VAT?

Karen: What do I expect? Oh, a holiday. Release from the chores. An unshackling of the chains, you know. Something, different. A bit of life. A bit of *unreality* to savour. To cherish when winter comes. A bit of sun to distil the grey. Find something. Perhaps just an affair . . . with a beginning, a middle and an end. For two weeks, a separate reality. That's all.

Rick: I hope you find it, kid. But it all comes at a price, you know. You only get what you pay for. And, darling, you're on the plebs beano. You're with the rabble. That's all you could afford. Keep yourself covered when you're on the beach. Don't mess about in churches if you take the sightseeing trips. Knock down every price the market mob ask when you're buying your souvenir castanets and Flamenco fans and don't drink the tap water. You sure you ain't a bunny girl?

Karen: That's about the most insulting thing anyone has said to me.

Rick: Sorry about that. Most of the other birds here'll be flattered.

Karen: I'm not most of the other birds here.

Rick: That's a pity. Be simpler if you were.

[*There is the sound of smashing glass, roars and police sirens from offstage*]

Karen: What's that?

Rick: That's our fellow countrymen enjoying themselves on the Costa Brava, love. The lads. Smashed out of their heads — if they ain't with a tart, they're vomiting and if they ain't vomiting they're dago-bashing or smashing up a bar. You should have seen it last week. Some daft tour operator booked in a mob from Manchester in with Southampton. Football fans. They smashed ten thousand pesetas' worth of plate glass, three in hospital and twenty seven arrests. They'll never learn. [*He stands*] That's the reality, love. Have a good holiday. [*He looks at her, and then goes*]

Karen: I'm not asking for paradise. . . . [*She goes as lights fade and music comes in — Amen Corner:* If Paradise is half as nice. *The music continues in blackout*]

Scene: **The patio next morning.** *The music fades as the lights come up to reveal brilliant sunshine. Several kids are scattered about the patio.* **Paula** *and* **Janet** *are lounging about on chairs/lilos.* **Al, Steve Tony** *and* **Sid** *are kicking a plastic football about and yelling. The ball hits* **Paula** *on the head.*

Al: Sorry darlin'. That was me banana shot.

Paula: You can stuff your banana shot.

Al: Fancy a drink?

Paula: You can't afford what I fancy.

Al: What hey.

Janet: No ball games on the patio. It says on the sign, no ball games on the patio. What was all that bloody noise last night — kept me awake.

Tony: You should have seen it. It was great. Coming back from the open air disco, smashed out of his head El Sid was—

Sid: Two bottles of Chablis, twelve Bacardis and — it was that bleeding mineral water that did me.

Tony: So we was bundling down the bleeding hill, weren't we, and Sid slips on his arse, going like a sledge, weren't he—

Sid: Right through the plate glass windows at the hotel. How did I know they'd closed the bloody door?

[*They laugh.* **Tony** *exits*]

Paula: So what happened?

Sid: Waiters went a bit spare, didn't they. Right ding dong. With that queer one with the moustache. [*Laughs*] He should be out out of hospital by Christmas.

Paula: You make me sick, you do. You make me sick.

Sid: Not my fault. I tell you, it was the mineral water.

[**Tony** *returns*]

Tony: Funny, no one serving in the bar.

Sid: I need a drink to clear my head. It's all fuzzy.

Tony: No one in reception either.

Al: Here, Carlos—

[*A waiter,* **Carlos,** *hurries by.* **Tony** *and* **Sid** *grab him*]

Sid: Where's everyone?

Tony: There's no one serving in the bar, no one in reception, and in the dining room all the—

Carlos: We have a meeting. Of all the hotel workers.

Al: You can't go clearing off to meetings when we're thirsty.

Carlos: Too bad. It is very serious. We have had no extra money for three summers. There may be a strike.

Al: A what?

Carlos: I'm in a hurry, I'll be late.

Al: I warn you, Carlos. Any strike, mate, and I'll use your head like a plug in me bath. Know what I mean?

Carlos: I want no trouble. We are all brothers in the cause of international—

Al: Don't you start that lark. I'm up to here with all that back home.

Tony: Listen Carlos, son—

[**Carlos** *retreats, then runs.* **Tony, Steve, Al** *and* **Sid** *chase him off*]

Paula: They wouldn't dare do it, would they?

Janet: And if they did, would we get a reduction?

[**Lynne** *and* **Ali** *enter, wearing bikinis*]

Lynne: Rub it good and proper across me shoulder blades. That's where it started peeling last year.

Ali: I'll put extra there.

Lynne: I'm sweltering already.

Ali: We'd better not overdo it today.

Lynne: An hour in the morning and then an hour in the afternoon. That's enough for the first day.

Ali: They say if you get too much sun you go senile before you're thirty.

Lynne: Who wants to be thirty? I want to be young forever.

[*They sit in empty beach chairs*]

Ali: Oh, this is the life.

Lynne: Yeah.

Ali: So peaceful.

Lynne: Yeah.

[Viva España *blares somewhere offstage.* **Tony, Steve, Sid** *and* **Al** *enter, cross the stage kicking their ball and singing with the music. They leave*]

Lynne: I'm cheesed off with that bloody song and I ain't been here a day yet.

Ali: I quite like it. [*Slight pause*] But not all the time. [*Pause*] I wonder where Helen and Karen are?

Lynne: Karen said she weren't going to leave the dining room until she got her breakfast. [*Pause*] She'll be there all night. They've already labelled her a right troublemaker. Oh, she's had it. She'll get less chips than everybody else and they'll load her omlettes with garlic. Till her eyes run. Serves her right if she's going to be difficult.

Ali: I was amazed when she said she was going to come. It's just not her sort of holiday. [*Pause*] Mind you, I can't imagine what is. She criticizes everything. I imagine there's been a great tragedy in her life.

Lynne: Why?

Ali: Oh, I dunno. She has the air of somebody who knows tragedy. Like a Georgette Heyer heroine. The one Crusaders always fancy like mad but her air of remoteness puts them off, so they go hunting dragons instead as a sexual relief. [*Pause*] Oh, this is the life.

[**Helen** *enters wearing an exotic beach gown*]

Helen: Bonsoir.

Lynne: That's 'good night' in French.

Helen: Oh, is it?

Lynne: You look like Petticoat Lane on a windy day.

Helen: Me mum made this out of the old bathroom curtains.

Lynne: How's the bathroom look? Hey, pull up a chair and sit down and get out of me sun, will you?

Helen: I'll sit on the floor.

Ali: Where's Karen?

Helen: She's having a terrible row with the waiter. It embarrassed me so much . . . I left. About her coffee being cold and a fascist dictatorship, or something. She said at least she thought fascists were efficient.

Lynne: For supper she'll have a hand-grenade pudding.

[**Karen** *enters*]

Helen: I don't think she likes it here much. When the porter showed us to our room last night, she made out she thought it was the broom cupboard.

Lynne: She's getting up my nose.

[**Karen** *stretches. She is wearing a bikini*]

Lynne: Hey, get out of my sun, will you?

Ali: You've already got a bit of a tan, Karen.

Karen: I went away at Easter. France.

Lynne: That's nice. Ernie come up?

Ali: I'm lucky if I can afford one holiday every two years.

Karen: I was working in a bar at night. In London. And a full-time job. That's how I afforded it.

Ali: Why did you come to Hull?

Karen: Where did our courier say he'd be?

Ali: I think he said the Hotel Splendida, why?

Karen: I want to find out about the excursions. I want to see Spain, not the tourists' stuff.

Lynne: You are a bloody tourist!

Karen: There's a castle on an island . . . just the castle. It covers the whole of the island. Somewhere. I'd like to go there, on a boat, slowly, in the early evening when the sun's going down.

Lynne: You won't get many Green Shield stamps for that. You try so bloody hard to be different, it gives me a headache.

Karen: I'm sorry about that.

Lynne: Can I ask you a personal question, seeing we're all so carefree and abandoned here. Why did you come to Hull? To Whitworth and Sons?

Karen: Why did Helen come — why don't you ask her? She's a Geordie, she's not—

Lynne: It was different for her—

Helen: Me dad had to go to Hull for his work, 'cause he lost his job, see—

Lynne: She had to, she had no choice. You did — why?

Karen: I don't think it's really any of your business, do you? [*As she goes, a lad makes a grab at her*] Try that again and I'll open your face with a bottle. [**Karen** *threatens, then leaves with dignity. There is amazement all round*]

Lynne: Right mistake asking her to come.

Helen: I couldn't believe it when she said yes.

Ali: I couldn't believe it when you asked her.

Lynne: God, I'd drunk too much or I never would have done.

Ali: That's peculiar — I wonder where all those waiters keep going?

Helen: Where—

Ali: Over there, in the table tennis room. Like a meeting or something.

[**Lynne** *gets up, goes to wave, but doesn't*]

Helen: What's—

Lynne: Nothing, I thought, but—

Ali: What is it, Lynne?

Lynne: Daft, from behind, that waiter looking like Alberto.

Ali: Oh.

Lynne: Crazy. [*She blows her nose loudly*]

Ali: Are you sure you're all right?

Lynne: Yeah, great [*She howls loudly – real tears*]

Helen: Lynne -- what is it?

Lynne: It's nothing.

Paula: Can you do nothing quieter, please.

Lynne: Shut your face, fatso.

Paula: Charming, in't it? The class of person you get here. I do hope the Spaniards don't get the wrong idea of the English.

Ali: What is it, Lynne? I've never seen you so upset.

Lynne: Just catching sight of that bloke, thinking it was him . . . brought it all back.

Helen: Who?

Lynne: Who do you think cloth ears – Alberto!

Helen: Oh, I'm sorry. Does he look like him then?

Lynne: Yeah, but Alberto was better looking. I had this . . . stupid dream, see . . . a couple of times . . . that when I stepped off the plane last night . . . he'd be there, waiting for me . . . with a bunch of flowers or sommat. Daft cow, ain't I. I said to meself, I hope you're not deluding yourself, girl. I hope you ain't going all the way to Spain on the off chance of seeing Alberto. [**Ali** *and* **Helen** *offer cigarettes*] He used to phone sometimes . . . reversed charges, me old man'd go mad. He said he was phoning up to say he was coming to live with me in Hull. He said he'd throw up everthing to be near me. He said he'd get a job in a Wimpy bar.

Ali: A Wimpy bar?

Lynne: He was particularly partial to Wimpys. Cheeseburgers. He said. He never came though. Still. Never mind.

Helen: No, never mind.

Lynne: Plenty more fish in the sea.

Ali: Shall we have a jug of whatsit then?

Lynne: Yeah, *sangría*. A great jug of it and three glasses.

Helen: OK. [*She gets up to go, then pauses*] Where do you go?

Lynne: Look the poolside bar over there. Where them two blokes are lolling about. Typical barmen.

Helen: All right. What shall I say?

Lynne: *Sangría*. Say *sangría*. Ino jugo – three persons. It's easy.

Helen: All right. I'd better put me beach coat on again in case I get touched up. It was terrible going across the foyer. It was like wrestling with an octopus.

Lynne: Put on a Captain Ahab raincoat and a pair of Wellington boots, all the difference it'll make. It's Spain see. The sun. You just ooze sex appeal. It comes out of you like insect repellent in reverse.

Helen: See you in a minute, then. . . .

Lynne: If any fellahs try it too hard, just shout *Fire!*

Helen: Fire?

Lynne: If you shout rape, everyone stands around and has a good laugh.

[**Helen** *goes, giggling. She shrieks before finally disappearing. Others laugh*]

Ali: Oh, this is the life.

Lynne: That's the twentieth time you've said that today.

Ali: Well, quarter to eleven ordering *sangría* and smoking these pongy fags, baking hot. I'll have a swim in a minute. [*She laughs*] This time, of a morning, I normally go to the Athene to get the elevenses for everyone. Eight coffees, three with, two without, one black with, six teas, two without, one with lemon and four danish pastries and a Bovril for old Mr Armitage. [*She laughs again. She stands and starts doing arm exercises*] Well, they can bloody well get their own today — and for the next twelve days. [*She laughs*] And they really get annoyed if I get them wrong. Miss Hart of costing typists went up the wall 'cause there was sugar in her tea. Wouldn't pay me for it. Weren't my fault. Sod Miss Hart. *Get it yourself today, you old bag.* That's what I say.

Lynne: What's all the exercise, kiddo?

Ali: Bust exercises. You can put on an inch a month if you do seven hundred of these a day.

[Viva España *suddenly booms out again as* **Tony**, **Steve**, **Sid** *and* **Al** *pass by. They stand around* **Ali** *doing identical exercises. They laugh as she becomes embarrassed*]

Lynne: Don't take the mick — buy us a drink.

Al: No chance — the bloody barmen have gone to a meeting.

Lynne: Oh, is that where they've gone. What for?

Sid: Carlos said there might be a strike.

Lynne: [*Leaping up*] A what!

Tony: Bloody strike. I tell you, if they dare go on strike they better book up their undertaker. Kill the lazy sods. I've never heard anything like it in all my life.

Ali: But that'd be terrible. We'd all die of starvation and thirst.

Al: We'll raid the kitchens, mate, smash down the shutters of the bars, help ourselves. You ladies can do the cooking and us lads could. . . .

Lynne: I'm not on holiday to cook.

Tony: What are you on holiday for, then?

Lynne: Take your hands off. They're all sweaty.

Ali: I didn't think they was allowed to go on strike in Spain.

Tony: Rick said there's been a few strikes in Madrid and Barcelona. The cops shot the sods.

Al: Bit strong.

Lynne: There must be somewhere to get a drink. Helen's trying over there—

Ali: Look at the queue!

Al: Anyhow, I'm a bit skint. I'm only on National Security, you know. [*He laughs*] Only kidding.

Tony: Here, catch a look at her.

[**Kitty** *enters. The lads follow her off*]

Ali: The one in the checked hat and braces looked nice.

Lynne: Bloody English. They never have no money.

Ali: I've never, you know, foreign fellah. . . .

Lynne: Oh, it's so different, Ali. They don't just grab you and start rubbing – they give you the bleeding kiss of life first. You just treat them like dirt and they worship you. [**Ali** *laughs and turns a cartwheel. There are whistles from offstage. She sits*] The thing is with dagos, don't let on that you like them. 'Cause then they'd have you cleaning their teeth. Keep them panting.

Ali: I shall.

Lynne: We'll have a swim in the sea later. Make out we've been attacked by jellyfish. That way we can take our pick as they dive in to rescue us. It's great. Last year I had an Algerian ice cream seller sucking me toes for half an hour. I never knew toes were so sexy.

Ali: That'd blow the buzzing out of Helen's ear 'oles.

Lynne: Can you see her?

Ali: Aye. Poor cow, way that Dave bloke treated her.

Lynne: She's so good, she hasn't even mentioned it. She's gonna enjoy herself. Bliss. Right?

Ali: Right.

Lynne: Only young once.

Ali: Make every minute count.

Lynne: Take it – everything that's offered.

Ali: And if it isn't offered–

Lynne: Steal it. [*They shake hands*] We're getting visually raped.

Ali: Where?

Lynne: Don't look. They're foreign all right. Not sweating off last night's beer like English fellahs. You can always tell. Sit down. Look casual. [*They sit, then lie.* **Andy** *enters carrying a camera*]

Andy: Would you like to expose yourselves to my Leica?

Ali: Beg your pardon?

Andy: Picture?

Lynne: Come back in a couple of weeks when we've got our tans.

Andy: I'll underexpose in me dark room. Make you look right dusky. A little bit of touching up with me fine badger's hairs.

Lynne: Get lost.

Ali: Not now.

Andy: OK. Probably wouldn't come out anyroad. Bloody Bradford mob kept saying back a bit, back a bit. Landed in the pool, didn't I? Hundred and eighty quid's worth of Leica here. Used a can of glycerine to stop me rollers rusting.

Ali: How tragic. Here, what's all this about this strike—

Andy: Oh, no chance. They're just playing silly buggers. Now the season's underway they think by threatening to go out they can get whatever they want. Out of the question. They'll chuck them all in the army. Serves them right. Oh, Rick—

Rick: [*Entering*] Hello, hello. [*He looks around for* **Karen**] Where's the rest of your mob?

Lynne: Round and about.

Andy: I've been having a bit of trouble with my clutch, Rick; I wonder if you could do it for us.

Rick: Bring it round this afternoon. . . . I'll ring up about the parts. [*To girls*] Where's the one with the red hair?

Lynne: Complaining about something. She's always complaining.

Rick: Are you lot mates?

Ali: We all work in the same office.

Rick: Funny, she don't look like a. . . . OK, Andy. This afternoon. [*Laughs*] They're talking about going on strike. Me bar'll be so crowded tonight I'll be able to retire. [*Laughs, exits*]

Lynne: He's a funny sort of bloke.

Andy: Great bloke during the day. But terrible when he's drunk. He gets drunk every night.

Ali: It can't be doing his kidneys any good.

[**Andy** *goes laughing. The girls lie back*]

Lynne: I feel like ... Brigitte Bardot and Miss World and Princess Margaret rolled into one and blasted with stardust. Irrrestible, I am irresistible! [*She leaps up*] Christ. Some bleeder's stung me. Size of that lump. Bleeding mosquito. And there's another one. It must be the coconut oil. It's down me pants. It's biting me to death. Hang about, hang about, I'll jump in the pool. [*She runs off towards the pool.* **Helen** *enters from the other side with a* **waiter** *carrying a tray of* sangría]

Ali: You took your time.

Helen: Oh, thank you, *muchas gracías*. Shall I tip him?

Ali: Oh, yeah.

Helen: How much?

Ali: I dunno.

Waiter: Twenty-five pesetas.

Ali: Oh, thank you.

Helen: I'll go and get the hot dogs. I ordered them. I barked and mimed it being hot. They understood. [*She goes, laughing, and happy*]

Ali: Hurry up, Helen, 'cause we ordered another jug from some Krauts and Lynne might no— [*The* **Waiter** *is stroking her back*] Oh — I thought all you waiters were going on strike.

Waiter: You are so tense ... relax, relax ... is that better?

Ali: Oh, it's lovely. Are you a right proper Spaniard; only you don't look very brown.

Waiter: That is because I have to work so hard to make enough money to be able to stay alive. Days, nights, no days off. . . . I have only one shirt which I must wash every night. Only two hours sleep. . . . I cannot even afford to buy myself a drink. . . .

Ali: Oh, have some of this.

Waiter: You are too kind, thank you [*He drinks some and sits closer to her. **Al**, **Sid**, **Tony** and **Steve** enter clapping their hands to a Chelsea chant. They surround the **Waiter**]*

Al: What's all this about a bloody strike then?

Waiter: It is just—

Tony: We didn't come all the way to Lloret to have you lot go on strike — there's enough of that back home.

Waiter: I'm sure you will enjoy yourselves.

Sid: Bloody right we will, mate.

Al: Give warning — any of this strike lark and there'll be none of you on your bloody feet to walk out on strike.

[*The lads take the jug out of his hands and knock him over. He gets up to run off but they trip him. He scampers off with the lads jeering after him*]

Ali: You stupid—

Tony: Ooooo, temper, temper—

Ali: Run away, you little children.

Steve: Now, now.

Ali: What was the point of that?

Tony: Bit of a laugh, just a laugh, in't it.

Steve: Dago, in't he—

Ali: Why don't you pick on them? They're dagos and all.

[*Two **Guardia** appear by the poolside. The lads look. The **Guardia** approach and look at the lads. Silence*]

Tony: [*In Dixon of Dock Green voice*] Hello, hello, hello. [*In Eric Morecambe voice*] It wasn't me, officer. It was that little fellah with the short hairy legs. He did it. I said to him — What do you think of the show so far and he said—

Lads: Rubbish.

[*They laugh. One of the* **Guardia** *holds* **Tony's** *face. He releases it and the two* **Guardia** *leave*]

Tony: Don't like Morecambe and Wise.

Steve: Bleeding shooters.

Al: Nasty sods.

Ali: Why don't you go dago-bashing the cops?

Tony: I'll give her the first ten reasons, then you take over, Sid.

[*The lads sit by* **Ali** *and help themselves to the* sangría]

Ali: Oooo, this is the life!

[*Loud music: the Stones'* Jumping Jack Flash. *The lights change to flashing disco lights and the stage fills with dancers*]

Scene: **A disco on the patio.** *It is night. There are disco lights, dancers, loud music. The disco ends and there is a spotlight on* **Pete**, *the courier, who is now the DJ. He wears an exotic costume. Using a mike, he makes an announcement.*

Pete: And now, now . . . thank you . . . bit of hush . . . bit of the non-verbals. . . . Right, further to your entertainment. . . we are proud to present, at great cost, the one and only. . . . *Alfredo.*

[*There are cheers and boos. Another spot on* **Alfredo**, *the Flamenco dancer. He looks white and miserable. He does a limping Flamenco to jeers, catcalls, laughs and the accompany-*

ing guitar music. At the end of the dance, someone throws a Pepsi-Cola can]

Alfredo: So kind, so kind. Plebs. [*He grits his teeth as the spotlight changes to full lights, revealing an almost empty stage. Just the pop group's instruments.* **Rod** *is alone, putting his guitar into its case.* **Helen** *enters*]

Helen: Been outside listening . . . you were really great.

Rod: Just rehearsing, you know.

Helen: Sounded fabulous. Saw you at Fat Cat's the other night, great.

Rod: Talent scout, are you?

Helen: Me?

Rod: Reviewer from the NME on a Costa del Sol junket?

Helen: No—

Rod: I know. Island Records Majorcan A and R man in disguise?

Helen: All I said was, I like your original numbers. Sorry I. . . . [*She turns to go.* **Rod** *catches her arm*]

Rod: Hey. Our originals, eh? At Fat Cat's, all they want us to do is hammer out the Stones and Beatles and all that crap. And poxy Viva Lasagna. [*She grins*]

Rod: Ssssh. [*Silence*] Hear it? That is silence. That is . . . silence. Drink it in, it doesn't come here very often. [*Pause*] Buy you a drink to celebrate.

[*They sit at a table.* **Rod** *shouts for a waiter*]

Helen: First time I heard you, I knew immediately that you was an English group.

Rod: Band.

Helen: Yes. 'Cause the Spanish bands—

Rod: Groups.

Helen: Oh, I see the difference. Well, the Spanish sing in English and that but they can't put it over like you can. You know they're Spanish especially when they do something like the Stones. [*Grunts can be heard offstage*] You speak Spanish?

Rod: Been here two years, ain't I?

Helen: Gosh.

Rod: Two bleeding years in this ponce of a place.

Helen: Don't you like it here?

[*He laughs.* **Rick** *enters, wearing a crumpled white suit*]

Rod: Hi, Rick. I like the new ventilation.

Rick: Flying beer bottles last night. Leeds United fans. Cheaper not to bother getting it fixed. Specially if we lose the Test match.

Helen: I don't know why they do it. It makes me so ashamed to be English.

Rick: I'd try not to worry about it too much, love. I mean, you are on holiday.

Helen: Why did you call your bar 'The Howling Budgie'?

Rick: I couldn't spell 'Canary'.

Helen: Do you like living here?

Rick: The sun makes everything better. Sun on your back, it's OK.

[**Karen** *enters.* **Rick** *grins*]

Karen: Have you seen our courier?

Rick: Sit down, I'll get you a drink.

Karen: Right now I'd like some coffee with my breakfast. Or a three-course lunch in the correct order.

Rick: I warned you when you got here. Plebs' beano. You sure you weren't a bunny?

Karen: Positive. [*She goes*]

Rick: [*Laughs*] Temper, temper. She looks like she's constipated. I'll get your drinks. [*He leaves*]

Helen: She doesn't seem to be enjoying herself very much.

Rod: And that's the point ain't it?

Helen: Yeah.

Rod: Let go, kiddo, let go. You'll regret it otherwise. Freest time of your life. When you're an old lady you'll lay in your geriatric ward and think: Lloret 1976. I wasted it. It'll be worse than death.

Helen: Yeah.

Rod: Come with your mates, did you?

Helen: Yeah. The girls I work with.

Rod: And they're at it all the time. [*Laughs*] I've seen you on your own, last thing, three o'clock in the morning in a corner of the disco, stretching out a Coke, checking your watch. Means you have to stay out of your bedroom till your mate's finished with her fellah, right?

Helen: Right.

Rod: You ought to put your foot down. You're paying half the rent.

Helen: Exactly.

Rod: You need a good night's kip.

Helen: I do, otherwise I'll go home needing a holiday.

Rod: What's your name?

Helen: Helen.

Rod: I'm Rod. Cheers. What's wrong then, Helen? Can I guess? Some guy back home, engaged or something . . . last minute he chickens out of it. So you come away with the girls from work to forget all about him and—

Helen: And . . . and I can't. [*She begins to cry.* **Rod** *comforts her.* **Rick** *enters with drinks*]

Rod: Poor cow. There always has to be one like her, don't there. [*He helps* **Helen** *off as* **Steve, Al, Tony** *and* **Sid** *enter*]

Rick: Come to put me window back in?

Steve: Oh, someone smashed your window, what a shame.

Rick: Yeah, great pity. That's why I doubled the price of your drinks last night – didn't you notice. Buy me a new window.

Steve: Bit steep—

Rick: What do you think I'm here for, charity?

Al: You must be making a packet.

Rick: Everyone comes here to toss their money away. OK – I'll smile, stay open all night if that's what they want. I don't mind taking your money. But – the only thing I don't like, right – is bother. [*He is menacing* **Tony**] 'Cause, see – when there's bother . . . the cops sometimes think it's simpler to close the place where there's bother. And that'd cost me plenty. And I'd get very annoyed about all that. Violent even. [*Pause*] I'm glad we understand each other.

Tony: It was only a bit of fun with the dagos.

Rick: Pick on someone your own size. These geezers only trying to make a bit of money like everyone else. They've got wives and kids – break their arms and their kids go hungry. So lay off.

Steve: You fancy your chances against all of us, Rick?

Rick: Want to try me?

[*Pause*]

Tony: We going to have a drink or what?

Rick: Let's all have a drink. What you having?

Tony: I wouldn't say no to that one in the yellow dress.

[*Laughter as* **Lynne** *and* **Ali** *enter*]

Tony: Anything you want, Betty?

Ali: Oh, him again. I hate W. C. Fields.

Tony: Oooo, not nice.

Sid: Belt up will you, Tony, you're getting on my plumbs with all that. Bona afternoon, *señoritas*. My name is Sid. For short, El Sid.

Lynne: All right, we'll have a drink. [*To* **Rick**, *sexily*] Hello. . . .

Rick: What do you want?

Lynne: Crème de menthe in a great glass of lemonado with chunks of ice and a splash of vodka—

Rick: And a plastic bucket to put it in? *Cerveza* for you lot?

Steve: Right.

[**Rick** *goes*]

Sid: What you bought then?

Lynne: Suede skirt. Real authentic Spanish.

Sid: Oh, nothing like the authentic stuff, that's what I say. That's what counts. That's what I do in my trade.

Ali: What are you?

Sid: Greengrocer. Only authentic spuds, only authentic.

[**Tony** *makes a grab at* **Ali**]

Ali: Oi. . . . There's a time and a place for everything, thank you.

Tony: Ooo, I know the place to put it, Betty, if you tell me the time.

Lynne: Bloody heat goes to their heads, don't it?

Tony: No. I work in a bakery.

Ali: Why ain't you got flowers in your hair?

Tony: Olé.

Lynne: Bakers never go hungry.

Tony: I'm a trainee pastry chef.

Sid: If you ever want any cost price rock cakes, ask Tony. [*Laughter*] Does your husband know you're here, eh?

Lynne: He's picking us up in his yacht next week. Been on a cruise.

Tony: Boat race and took the wrong turn, eh?

Ali: Aren't they witty, Lynne?

Lynne: Just like 'Talk of the North', Ali.

Tony: Do your mates call you Muhammad?

Ali: Call that funny?

Tony: Right. There's this Irishman and he says to God: 'Oh God, why did you give oil to the Arabs and potatoes to the Irish?' And God said: 'The Irish had first choice.'

Lynne: Great, in't it. Come all the way to Spain to hear Irish jokes.

Ali: I don't get it.

Tony: Glad they let her out for the holiday. [*Laughter which freezes as the* **Guardia** *pass.* **Rick** *enters with a tray and curses under his breath at the* **Guardia**] Lot of it about.

Sid: Those bloody hats.

Tony: Like Ascot.

Rick: Those guns aren't toys. . . . Leave the waiters alone. You're . . . we're all on the same side.

Sid: All right Rick, give it a rest. We're on bleeding holiday. [**Rick** *goes and the kids drink*] Smashed.

Tony: He's always smashed.

Al: Cheers.

Scene: **A disco.** *The music continues; there is dancing. The kids join in with the singing; dance exotically; pour wine over each others faces from funnel bottles. During the dancing various snatches of conversation can be heard.*

Andy: Polaroid, colour transparency or black and white eight by ten in a gilt frame?

Paula: Big colour one.

Andy: All right in line, all you lot — together. Smile, smile.

Paula: Go on, then.

Janet: Say cheese.

Andy: No, say sex.

Paula: Sex?

Andy: It makes you show more teeth.

Tony: It makes you show more bleeding teeth.

Paula: Ooooooo.

[**Andy** *takes the pictures; nothing happens. They groan.* **Andy** *inspects his camera. The bulb flashes in his eyes*]

Andy: That'll bring on me migraine.

[*A drum roll and a spotlight comes on* **Peter** *who holds his microphone*]

Pete: Bit of hush, bit of hush. Now, my lords, ladies and gentlemen — and in-betweens. [*Applause*] But first a very serious announcement. The manager of Hotel Don Quixote has a request. They do not wish to report this to the Guardia because the consequences would be very serious. All they want is it's return. And no questions will be asked. Do I make myself understood?

Voice: What do they want returned?

Pete: Those who stole it know what I'm talking about. Suffice to say it's Spanish, weighs about sixteen stone and answers to the name of Matilda. [*Roars*] I can't think why anyone should want to steal a forty-five-year-old bedroom maid, but here you are. If you've dumped her in an airing cupboard or a lift shaft, may I just remind you — stealing women is a crime in Spain.

[**Karen** *steps into the spotlight and snatches* **Pete's** *microphone*]

Karen: First I have an announcement. I am a resident of this hotel and I wish to draw attention to something else which has been stolen.

Voices: Oi, oi. Get 'em off.

Karen: It weighed ten stone and answered to the name of Carlos. A waiter. Only there is no doubt who stole him. He was stolen by Guardia, this afternoon, taken away. [*Two* **Guardia** *appear on the edge of the stage*] We should ask questions, demand explanations, disrupt the spectacle. Or are we simply pawns who by being here make this hideous fascist state appear respectable? If we — [*Uproar.* **Rick** *steps into the spotlight and pulls her away*] Leave me alone, you're the most despicable of them all — you work here.

Pete: [*With microphone*] All a technical hitch, that. Thank you, Joan of Arc. And now, if you'd all like to move to the pool area, you will witness the stunning beauty of Spain's premiere topless limbo dancer — Señorita Sexyvilla.

[*Roars and jeers. All, except* **Karen** *and* **Rick***, leave towards the pool. Pasadoble music plays, the* **Guardia** *have gone and they are alone*]

Karen: The sods. They think they can get away with anything.

Rick: They can, mate. Fact of life. Carlos was the rabblerouser, calling meetings, bother, talking about a strike. That's the game here — risk your arm, they break it.

Karen: I don't know how you can live with that.

Rick: As long as the cash till keeps ringing.

Karen: Is that what it's all about?

Rick: Give me a better reason.

Karen: You're despicable.

Rick: I just want peace and quiet.

Karen: A great place for peace and quiet this is! All bloody 'Viva España' and the sound of pigs vomiting.

Rick: I thought Puking was a town in China till I came to Lloret. [*He laughs*]

Karen: That was moderately amusing.

Rick: Oh, thanks a lot. Have a drink—

Karen: I can't afford your prices.

Rick: On the house.

Karen: That's a bit out of character, isn't it?

Rick: It's me birthday. [*He leads her to a table, snaps his fingers, and a* **Waiter** *appears*] Scotch and—

Karen: Scotch.

[*The* **Waiter** *nods and goes*]

Rick: You're not a package tour bird.

Karen: I wanted to see Spain. It's all I could afford. I go on day trips.

Rick: Should have toured in a car.

Karen: I haven't got one.

Rick: Hitched?

Karen: I'd have been raped.

Rick: You have to pay for what you want.

Karen: Why did you used to run up the hill in seven and a half minutes?

Rick: Someone told me exercise was a kind of anaesthetic.

Karen: For what?

Rick: It's a long time ago.

Karen: What is?

Rick: This is a better one. [*The **Waiter** enters, puts glasses on the table and goes*] You enjoyed your trips then?

Karen: Yes.

Rick: Who do you go with?

Karen: On my own.

Rick: Haven't seen you for days. . . .

Karen: I hate it here. But outside the city. . . . Spain really does have . . . dignity and splendour and majesty and passion. . . . I don't know why they endure the indignity of this noise and candyfloss—

Rick: It puts food in bellies.

Karen: How long have you been here?

Rick: Years.

Karen: Why?

Rick: The sun makes everything OK.

[*Pause*]

Karen: There's a lot of places you can go for the sun.

Rick: This is cheap. *Mañana,* they say. Tomorrow, tomorrow — everything can wait till tomorrow. But here, tomorrow never comes. I like that.

Karen: A suspension of time — or reality?

Rick: [*Laughing*] You make me laugh. Do all people always say to you — don't worry it might never happen?

Karen: There's a castle, I read about it. I'd like to see it. Salvador Dali's castle. He bought it for his wife, but she'll only let him enter it with a written invitation — that she must write. He hires Catalan choirs to serenade her.

Rick: I've got a motor . . . could take you there, Port Lligat.

Karen: You'll lose money if you close for the day.

Rick: I'll get someone to work it for me.

Karen: I might not let you have me.

Rick: You can pay half the petrol then.

Karen: I don't like people like you.

Rick: That's all right then.

Karen: Do you never get involved?

Rick: It's cheaper. I'll be waiting in the foyer of your hotel — nine in the morning. OK.

[*There is a screech of tyres and the banging of car doors.* **Carlos** *enters pushed by two* **Guardia** *who then leave.* **Tony**, **Steve**, **Al** *and* **Sid** *enter and gather round* **Carlos**. **Carlos** *screams something at them.* **Rick** *leads* **Karen** *off, away from the scene*]

Al: Did you over, did they? Serves you right. You sticky-fingered Spaniard.

Steve: Lazy bleeder.

Tony: Keep your hands off the English girls, right?

Steve: We're paying for this bloody holiday. The girls are ours.

[*The lads push* **Carlos** *around. During this* **Rick** *re-enters and stands between* **Carlos** *and the boys*]

Rick: Leave him alone you stupid sods. Can't you see he's already been done once. . . ?

[**Carlos** *speaks quickly in Spanish*]

Al: What did he say?

Rick: He said he'd rather be dago-bashed by the English than the Guardia.

Al: Well, tell him — and tell him to tell all his mates — leave the girls alone or he'll get done again.

[*There is a pause.* **Rick** *stands motionless.* **Al** *flicks open a knife and threatens* **Rick**]

Rick: Why don't you just push off?

[*There is a pause then the lads slowly begin to leave.* **Karen** *enters and speaks to* **Rick**]

Karen: [*To* **Rick**] Tomorrow. Nine. [*She goes.* **Rick** *helps* **Carlos** *to his feet as the lights begin to fade*]

Rick: Come on Carlos, mate . . . let's find a doctor for you. . . .

[*They slowly leave; the lights continue to fade and the sounds of smashing glass and police sirens can be heard somewhere offstage*]

Act 2

Scene: **The hotel patio at night.** *The music played during the interval was Rodrigo's Guitar Concerto. Before the lights come up for the second half, the Stones' Fool to Cry is played. When the lights come up the patio is empty; coloured lights twinkle offstage. Giggling is heard, then* **Rod** *and* **Helen** *enter, their jeans rolled up around their knees.* **Rod** *carries his guitar.*

Helen: That water was still warm — two o'clock in the morning and the sea's still warm?

Rod: You shouldn't have gone in the sea at night.

Helen: Sharks?

Rod: Dago-bashing English with spear guns. [*He sits on the floor.* **Helen** *sits near him*]

Helen: This is nice.

[*He strums for a moment, then stops*]

Rod: Request time.

Helen: Oh – tell you what I did used to like – no, better not, it makes me sound right old-fashioned.

Rod: Tell me, Helen. . . .

Helen: Well, when I was a kid . . . loved it, this song . . . used to feel like it was me who was trying to do it . . . running along the beach at home, in the winter, when there was no one around, really cold – just me . . . trying to . . . well, 'Catch the Wind'. Do you know it?

Rod: Sing then. Don't be shy . . . and no one around except the stars and your shells and us.

[*He strums and they sing*]

Rod and Helen: 'In chilly hours and minutes of uncertainty
I want to be
In the warm heart of your loving mind
To feel you all around me
And to take your hand, along the sand
Ah, but I may as well, try and catch the wind.

'When sundown pales the sky
I want to hide behind your smile
And everywhere you look your eyes will find
To be with you now would be the sweetest thing
Would make me sing, ah but I may as well
Try and catch the wind.

'When rain has hung the leaves with tears
I want you near to kill my fears
To help me to leave all my blues behind
Standing in your heart is where I want to be
I long to be
Ah but I may as well try and catch the wind.'

[*Silence.* **Helen** *leans against him and he holds her*]

Helen: Best night of the holiday, this. [*Pause*] Goes so quick now . . . only three days to go . . . time racing. [*Pause*] I'll never forget tonight . . . getting away from Lloret . . . that restaurant . . . open air . . . fish cooked in salt . . . and – I'm really glad you didn't have to work tonight.

Rod: They prefer the DJ night anyway. They only have us 'cause we come cheaper than paying record royalties.

Helen: You hate the group, playing the disco, don't you?

Rod: Come here, being a wandering minstrel you know . . . played in Mac's bar . . . music of the mountains, 'Guantanamera' – when the Guardia weren't around – Rodrigos Guitar Concerto . . . all that. Bloody Germans used to get tanked up on *cerveza* and drowned me out with their bleeding marching songs . . . jacked it in.

[*They pause.* **Rod** *strums briefly, then stops. They can hear the sea*]

Helen: Haven't got this one. . . .

Rod: They'll charge you excess baggage – all your shells. What is it?

Helen: I think it's a sunset shell – I'll have to look it up in me book. It's the right size to be a sunset shell – 'cause of the colour, see – the pink rays. Like a sunset.

Rod: How do you know all about them?

Helen: Me dad. Always brought home shells for me. Fishing fleet, see.

Rod: That's a rotten job.

Helen: 'Tis now he's getting older. Hard graft, all weathers. He wouldn't like you—

Rod: Lazy . . . what?

Helen: Aye. Why did you come – I mean, didn't you never work properly?

Rod: Commuter, clerk, you know . . . near Liverpool Street. Waiting at the station one morning, to go to work . . . suit and that. . . .

Helen: Can't imagine you in a suit.

Rod: Sun was shining, start of a summer . . . here comes the sun, I thought. [*He plays the intro of* Here Comes the Sun. *Laughs*] Went home, packed a bag, passport OK, so – come. Two years ago . . . waiter at first . . . then when Rick knew I could play, gigged in the bars . . . this fellah come . . . big ideas for starting a group . . . Steve, Ray, them. Stayed.

Helen: I thought you were a right raver—

Rod: Raver. What a word. [*Laughs*] Well, give you the spiel. Thought you was like all the rest. We're crap.

Helen: You'll have to do something though, a job or—

Rod: Why?

[*Silence*]

Helen: I dunno.

Rod: You make me laugh.

Helen: Oh, I wish I could be like you . . . jack in things and wander off and not worry about nothing. . . .

Rod: Undertakers love worriers.

Helen: That's what Dave used to say—

Rod: He your fellah then?

Helen: Aye, were . . . he lost his job, see, they're closing down so many firms up there . . . home . . . and we were supposed to be getting wed. . . . September . . . everything was booked up . . . and one night he just never came round . . . so I went round to his mum, and she said he'd gone off. . . . Me dad said he'd kill him. . . . I thought he might have told me he was going. [*Pause*] It was Lynne's idea. I work with her, see – she said come to Spain with us and forget all about Dave. I . . . I can't, though.

Rod: He your only guy?

Helen: Aye, well . . . only proper one . . . only one I went all the way with . . . I went on the Pill for him. [**Rod** *laughs*] Don't laugh at me.

Rod: [*Laughing*] I'm not. . . . Come up to the house tonight.

[*She looks at him*]

Helen: The other fellahs—

Rod: Night off – they're all in Barcelona. Air hostesses, push-overs.

Helen: I dunno. . . .

Rod: Too young for widow's weeds.

Helen: I might find at the last minute I can't bring myself to do it.

Rod: I'll be gentle.

Helen: Yeah . . . you are gentle.

[*He rolls her on her back and kisses her*]

Rod: You're trembling.

Helen: I know, grief, all them stars. . . . Show me . . . all you know . . . do everything to me . . . I'm only young once.

Rod: Relax.

Helen: I can't relax when people tell me to relax.

Rod: Think cool things. [*He kisses her again.* **Lynne** *enters*]

Lynne: Helen—

Rod: Hell, it's Mary Queen of the Scotch.

Lynne: What you been doing all night?

Helen: We've been walking on the beach.

Lynne: Bloody beach. Coming all the way to Lloret and you go for a walk on the beach — you might have well stayed at home.

[**Rod** *and* **Helen** *have disengaged themselves.* **Al** *enters behind* **Lynne**]

Al: Ooo Lynne, they've been rude.

Lynne: What a night, eh? [*Sits crosslegged*] Talk about double helping of laughs. More like a chip butty of disasters.

Al: This yours? Play it? [**Al** *strums guitar badly*]

Lynne: Guess what?

Helen: What?

Lynne: I saw him!

Helen: Alberto?

Lynne: Aye, Al-bloody-berto. I treated him like an empty box of Colonel Sanders's chicken and chips. I kicked him in the gutter. Dead nonchalant, weren't I, Al.

Al: Right. Bit out of order he was, bit out of order. Seen any bullfights? We're going tomorrow. El Sid's gonna chuck the courier in the ring. [*Laugh*] Harr harr.

Lynne: Shut up will you, Al. Take no notice of Al here. He's dead worried. He's got four endorsements and he's getting done for drunk and driving the day after he gets home.

Al: Through a red light at seventy. The copper said blow in here so quick as a flash I says: 'Why, your hands cold?' Harr harr.

Lynne: Alberto said he'd lost me address. I said that's a bit bloody peculiar — you phoned me up often enough. Reversed charges and all.

Al: West Indies declared at 317 for 4, so I heard.

Lynne: I felt like taking me clogs off and hammering him. Oh, it was embarrassing, the way he was fawning all over me. It was pathetic. He was groping Ali like no one's business — making out he was a right Casanova. She was taken in, but he couldn't fool me.

Rod: It's getting cold.

Al: Here, if you ever want any cost price racket holds, ring me in Dagenham.

Lynne: And — what about Karen?

Helen: What?

Lynne: Definitely a mistake asking her to come. She's only a copy typist — and a temp — lording it over everyone.

Helen: I haven't seen her for a few days.

Lynne: It's that barman bloke, in't it. The flash sod, Rick or whatever. Right strange one he is.

Rod: You sound like Minnie Caldwell.

Lynne: I speak me mind. Something funny about him.

Rod: He runs a bar here. Makes bread. Happy, so what.

Lynne: There was a Great Train Robber who looked just like him.

Rod: Aw, shut up.

Lynne: I can smell a rat. He's no good, that's for sure. He's running away from something—

Rod: Maybe you.

Lynne: Any more of that and I'll set El Sid on you.

Rod: Listen, he's a good bloke. Why ever he's here, it's none of our business. What Karen does, is her business.

Lynne: It's disgusting – he's years older than her.

Rod: You, the fastest drawers on the Costa Brava – and – come on, Helen, let's go.

Lynne: Oh, I see, Miss Butter Wouldn't Melt in her Mouth is at it at last.

Helen: Lynne. I'm on holiday, I can do what I want.

Lynne: I do what I want.

Rod: Right. Everybody does what they want and everybody's happy.

Lynne: Happy? Here I am smothered from head to foot with mosquito bites and me guts rotting with all that oily food and – five years, no one'll want to know me so – I don't give a pinch of pig-shit if anyone thinks I'm an old bag.

Helen: I'm sure no one would dream of thinking such a thing, Lynne.

Lynne: I don't care if they do. Back home, see them women on the fish stalls. . . . Thirty-five and they look a hundred and twenty. Fat and grey and shiny skin and hair like Brillo pads. See them collecting their kids from the school at four o'clock and you wonder who'd give them a kid. I don't want to be ugly . . . worn out . . . old. . . . I know it's only a holiday . . . but I do so much wish it could be like this forever . . . know what I mean?

Al: I remember. . . . [*Pause; all the others look at him*] The time I remember wishing it'd stay the same forever was the summer holidays at school. . . . Sun always shone and the days never ended. . . . We'd ride our bikes along the Arterial, lorries racing by, we'd turn the bikes into them so the lorries'd

brush our elbows ... for the thrill. Sometimes the drivers'd
stop and scream, so we'd turn off the road and ride the hills
on the dumps. ... There was tiddlers in the rain puddles and
packing cases to hide in and drain pipes to crawl through ...
and then, near the end of the holiday.... Ford's close ... and
all the dads'd be home ... then it was the best time.... They'd
open the furnaces at the factory and clean them and the heat
would keep the sky red for days and nights. [*Pause*] I remember them holidays very well.... [**Lynne** *takes his arm*]

Lynne: We going to Fat Cat's then?

Al: Yeah ... only three nights to go....

Lynne: You coming?

Helen: Yeah ... but.... [*She looks at* **Rod**] But not to Fat
Cat's. [**Lynne** *nods, then turns and leaves with* **Al.** **Rod** *picks
up his guitar and faces the other direction, ready to leave.*
Helen *slowly picks up her bag and shoes*] You will ... be
gentle?

[*Pause, then* **Rod** *grins*]

Rod: Don't forget your shells....

[**Helen** *collects her shells and follows him off as lights fade.
Then loud music: Jeff Beck's* Hi Ho Silver Lining]

Scene: **The disco.** *The music continues loudly as the lights
change to disco lights. The stage fills with dancers. The music is
turned off at alternate verses and lines whilst the dancers sing the
words.*

Disc: 'You're everywhere and nowhere baby,
        That's where you're at,

Driving through the country hillside,
In your hippy hat.
And it's—'

All: 'Hi ho silver lining—'

Disc: 'Everywhere you go and baby—'

All: 'Outside the sun is shining—'

Disc: 'But I don't make a fuss, 'cause it's obvious'.

[At the end of the record a spotlight falls on **Peter** *in his exotic disc jockey garb: a matador's suit of tights, a Batman cape and a frogman's mask and snorkel. The crowd jeer as he shouts through the microphone]*

Peter: OK, boys and girls . . . and now . . . and now . . . quiet please. . . . Sleep well, for tomorrow we have the excursion to end all excursions — at very little extra charge — the coaches will be here in the afternoon to transport you across land to Plaza de Toros de Barcelona!

All: Oi, ooo!

Sid: Nice one, Cyril.

Peter: Or if you prefer it in *Inglés* — the Bullfight! *[A trumpet fanfare]* And just a few words of warning, not that I want to sound like a petty minded sub-postmistress, but — in España, bullfighting is a *Very Serious Lark*. Seriously verily. So, no pissing about. And I mean that. You are very lucky, you children of the sun. For the star turn is none other than — Diego Peurta! Now if any of you are a bit on the squeamish side, no go, no go. And another thing, this concerns the ladies. If the matador should chop off one of the bull's ears and chuck it at you — I don't want none of you fellahs chucking beer bottles at him. In retaliation. Tossing a bull's ear at a señorita means . . . well, it's a compliment. It means he likes the look of you. So take it as a compliment, and that's all. No repetition of last month's Bradford mob. That is, do I make myself clear . . . no ripping off your panties and hurling them at him. There's a good chance she'll be released at Christmas. You have been warned. You'll get your tickets on the coach which leaves at nine-thirty to take in a sightseeing tour of the cathederal, the Museo de Arte de Catalune and the shopping centre of the Plaza.

[*He is drowned out by new music: Faces'* Stay With Me. *This is followed by* Music of the Mountains *and other such gentle music which plays through until the end of the scene. The lights change to reveal evening on the patio. There are strings of coloured lights, and couples sitting at the tables – which have been set whilst* Peter *was in the spotlight.* Peter *wanders among the tables and stops to talk with one of the couples.* Andy *is at another table selling pictures*]

Paula: You mean to say one of your pictures actually come out!

Andy: I'm not a total berk.

Paula: How much is it?

Andy: Two hundred fifty pesetas that one.

Paula: But there's a great shadow across me face.

Andy: That's why you're getting it cheap.

Paula: I don't think I've got two hundred fifty pesetas to spare – I've got to buy presents for me mum and dad yet.

[Ali *and* Alberto *enter. They stop at the table where* Karen *sits alone writing*]

Ali: Karen – I thought you'd drowned or something!

Karen: Hello–

Ali: Christ, what a fantastic colour you've got. . . . I've just gone red – it's agony.

Karen: Want a drink?

Ali: Yeah, hey – this, this is Alberto.

Karen: THE Alberto?

Ali: Yeah.

Karen: Hello.

Alberto: Hello.

Ali: You haven't seen Lynne have you. . . ?

Karen: No.

Ali: Trying to keep out of her way . . . bit difficult, though, sharing the same room.

Alberto: Lynne, she hit me on the head with a clog.

Ali: Show the bump, Alberto.

Alberto: It is not so important.

Ali: She went barmy.

Karen: Does it hurt?

Alberto: Only when the English boys hit me on the head with bottles.

Ali: They're right bleeders ain't they?

[*Glass smashes offstage and roars are heard.* **Sid** *and his mob race across the stage shouting. As they leave, a* **Waiter** *with blood on his head enters, stops and shouts.* **Alberto** *shouts something at him in Spanish. They go to leave*]

Alberto: A bad cut . . . glass. . . . I see it get treated. *Momento.*

Ali: OK.

[**Alberto** *and the* **Waiter** *go*]

Karen: Why do they do it?

Ali: I dunno. It's terrible. It makes you feel so ashamed. Alberto keeps saying why, why, why? I can't explain.

Karen: No.

Ali: Alberto says: 'Why do they treat us like dogs and yet treat real dogs so well?' Something'll happen.

Karen: What do you mean?

Ali: Alberto says: 'You taunt a bull only so many times and then the bull charges.'

Karen: Yes. . . . You look very happy.

Ali: I am. Only three nights to go . . . I feel terrible, for Lynne. I can't help it really. . . . Alberto . . . strange. What are you doing?

Karen: Diary . . . writing it all down . . . so I don't forget it.

Ali: Haven't seen you for days, where you been?

Karen: With Rick . . . seeing places. . . . We stayed in Barcelona a couple of days. . . .

Ali: Must be fabulous . . . seeing all the places – someone showing you round who really knows the place . . . not just a courier.

Karen: Can't Alberto show you?

Ali: I asked him, but he won't. . . . Doesn't it seem funny?

Karen: What?

Ali: Well, I mean. . . . Rick . . . bit old isn't he?

Karen: Does it matter?

Ali: No . . . you prefer older people, do you? I mean, I can't imagine you with young fellahs somehow. . . . When you came to Whitworth and Sons . . . no messing about with the fellahs. Do you mind if I ask you something?

Karen: What?

Ali: I said to Lynne, I mean we thought – is there a great tragedy in your life? [**Karen** *laughs*] Sorry. Only I've never heard you talk about your mum or your dad or–

Karen: [*Lights a cigar*] Rick took me to a fish auction in Rosas. He actually did know some of the fishermen. Sometimes, they bring him their outboard motors to mend.

Ali: He mended Andy's car—

Karen: Tomorrow, Rick says he'll take me to the castle—

Ali: The one on the island?

Karen: No, that's a fairy story. . . . Salvador Dali's castle. In Port Lligat. Rick says he's seen him walking in the village . . . and seen through the windows of the castle. . . . Dali's got Al Capone's Cadillac, and around his swimming pool, there's green knitted grass made from wool and rooms full of busts of Roman emperors and stuffed bears and giraffes and a dancing nun and clockwork Chinese musicians.

Ali: I saw a programme about him — on the 'Russell Harty Show'.

Karen: I want to see it for real.

Ali: You are funny. You just don't want to be normal, do you?

Karen: I hope we see him.

[**Rick** *enters. He is a bit drunk*]

Rick: We'll have to be up early.

[*Another crash and a roar somewhere offstage*]

Ali: Oh God — they're going mad . . . somewhere. . . .

Rick: The bloody idiots . . . they go on and on and then they find themselves in a corner where there's no getting out.

Karen: You're shivering—

Rick: Oh—

Karen: You are.

Rick: I . . . hate that senseless violence. . . . There seems enough without looking for it. [*Pause*] Ever seen a head go through a windscreen? Ever seen firemen cutting a woman out of a tangled wreck after a car smash? It makes all this . . . seem a bit excessive. How's the scribbling?

Karen: Oh, OK.

Rick: Chapter Two — going to be a book is it?

Karen: Maybe.

Ali: She's always writing at work.

Rick: What's it about?

Karen: The irrational attraction between two unalike people.

Rick: Many laughs?

Karen: You really are frightened, aren't you?

Rick: Not of their dago-bashing — of what's going to happen when the dagos bash back. They know what real violence is all about. For Christ's sake — we're almost in Basque country here. [*Drinks.* **Alberto** *enters*] How is he?

Alberto: A bottle, in his eye.

Ali: Oooo.

Alberto: Why?

Rick: Been like that since they stopped getting free milk at school?

Alberto: They think we're savages, Rick? They think we stay here, wait at their table, serve their drinks so that they put bottles in our face? Kick us? Ten on to one? Henriques last month — he *still* in hospital. He has wife and children in Barcelona. Now he cannot work for the rest season. Is that funny?

Rick: No, it ain't funny.

Alberto: I do not understand it. They are all two different people. One minute they laugh with us, jokes and buy drinks.

Another minute, they surround us . . . so much hate in their
eyes. . . . There will be terrible, terrible trouble — we not
take it all.

[**Carlos** *enters*]

Carlos: The doctor is coming.

Alberto: Good.

Carlos: Rick, you are English — you must tell the English
boys that it is too dangerous to—

Rick: Nothing to do with me, mate — you tell them.

Carlos: They are your countrymen—

Rick: I left that country.

Karen: But you could at least—

Rick: I've got me own problems.

Karen: You can't just stand by and—

Rick: Why not? I'm sorry, Carlos — I'm not getting involved.
You've sorted it out before, you sort it out again.

[*Pause*]

Carlos: I'm disappointed with you, Rick.

Rick: Yeah, well, I'm only trying to make an honest living.

[**Carlos** *goes. There is a pause*]

Karen: Do you never get involved in anything distasteful?

Rick: Look, I serve them kids their booze. I don't have to pay
them in kind, do I? They've had enough warnings. OK they've
got to learn what it's all about. Like we all have to learn.
They reckon they can terrorize, OK let them find out what real
terror is about. It'll be a blow for all those poor sods back
home who get done over every time Chelsea or Manchester

United lose. [**Helen** *and* **Rod** *enter, arms round each other, jeans rolled up, carrying shells*] You go in that sea much more often, you'll start bleeding shrinking.

Helen: Hello, hello, hello. . . .

Rick: [*Shouts off*] We need some more glasses.

Karen: And *sangría*.

Ali: I'm almost broke. I've only got ten pounds left and I haven't bought me mum's present yet.

Rick: It's on me. I had a bit of luck on the gee gees.

Ali: You look fantastic, Helen, all your hair's gone silver.

Helen: Aye.

Karen: What have you got?

Helen: Look. The beach is so fabulous. . . . so huge some of the shells. Looks like a duck's plumage.

Ali: That's beautiful, that one.

Helen: The colour looks like an egg, so yellow, and see that – the way it was eating the red sponge.

Ali: How many you got now?

Helen: Tons.

[*A* **Waiter** *enters and serves drinks*]

Ali: What is it?

Rick: A . . . delicacy.

[*The* **Waiter** *goes*]

Ali: Great. I'm very partial to delicacies. So smashing – all being together again. Well, almost–

Helen: How is Lynne?

Ali: She's been a bit ill . . . food poisoning, I think.

Helen: And mosquito bites.

Ali: Yes . . . she does seem unlucky.

Alberto: She hit me on the head with a clog.

Ali: Show her the bump, Alberto.

Alberto: It is not so important. You have your guitar, Rod?

Rick: Yes, what's happened with your *real* music? When are you coming to serenade my patrons again?

Rod: Off season — safest.

Karen: Salvador Dali hired a Catalan choir to serenade his wife.

Rod: Who won't let him in her castle?

Karen: You know about that?

Rod: Keep wanting to go and see it—

Karen: Can't they come with us tomorrow, Rick?

[*The* **Waiter** *enters with plates of fish*]

Rick: Why not? — Ah, food.

Ali: Fantastic!

Helen: What are they?

Waiter: *Centolla!*

Rod: Crab—

Ali: Great, fantastic — oh, this is the best night of the holiday—

Helen: Yeah.

Rick: Just tear it off and eat it with your fingers.

Ali: This is really delicious, this is fabulous.

Helen: Yeah. . . . Hey, come on, Rod . . . while it's quiet . . . give us a tune.

Ali: Yeah.

Rod: No.

Helen: He always says no the first time. You have to ask him twice.

[*They laugh*]

Karen: Come on, Rod.

Rod: What, then? [*He strums the chords of a song. As he begins to sing,* **Lynne** *enters, all her exposed skin speckled with white powder*]

Lynne: Great. How cosy. Glad you're all having a smashing time. All right Alberto, don't run off. You look like a petrified turtle, you cowering git.

Alberto: Lynne, dear Lynne—

Lynne: Don't try none of that soft soap on me. It won't wash. I'm surprised at you Ali, honest I am. You've borrowed your last pair of sling-backed shoes off me. When we get back to Whitworth and Sons I'll give you bloody hell.

Ali: What's the matter with you — all that white stuff?

Lynne: Irresistible, ain't I? To mosquitoes and gnats and as far as giant bees are concerned, I'm the best thing since strawberry jam. [*She sits: her hand is bandaged*]

Ali: Did a giant bee do that to your hand?

Lynne: No, fell over, didn't I? Smashed out of me head on Bacardi and lime and I fell into a cactus bed. I couldn't get up. There's only one poisonous cactus on the Costa Brava, the doctor said. That's the one me hand landed on. Pity, it's me bloody bingo finger.

Ali: Would you like some crab?

Lynne: No, thank you very much. No solids for two days. They tried to poison me in the Zaragosa Bar. I can't hold nothing down. And they had chips this afternoon on the menu. Don't laugh, it's not funny.

Ali: I know — I'm sorry — I—

Lynne: I'm surprised at you, Helen, I thought you might have shown some concern. Not that you've been near the hotel to notice. Pity, you might have got this sooner.

Helen: What is it?

Lynne: Telegram, isn't it. For you!

Helen: A telegram, Christ!

Lynne: Don't worry, can't be nothing tragic. It's a greetings telegram. I think the GPO have some regulations preventing them sending tragic news on cheerful cards.

Helen: Oooo.

[*They look at her*]

Rod: What's the matter Helen. . . ?

Helen: It's from . . . Dave. . . .

Rod: Aye.

Helen: Says . . . he says. . . . [*She begins to cry*]

Lynne: Well don't keep us all in suspense. Has he won the pools or hooked the Loch Ness monster?

Helen: Says. . . . You read it Rod, I can't. . . .

Rod: 'Come back Stop Wedding on again Stop I love you Stop Dave.'

[*Silence, then* **Helen** *runs off*]

Lynne: You better follow her – make sure she don't do nothing silly like sticking her head in a half pint of lager.

[**Rod** *goes*]

Karen: You ought to be in the diplomatic corps, Lynne.

Lynne: Oh, aye. Telegram for her, so—

Karen: You might have guessed what it was. Why make it bad for her when she's happy?

Lynne: Happy, is she?

Ali: Can't you see it, Lynne? She's really in . . . love . . . with Rod.

Lynne: Love, what's that? Love's two Bacardi and Cokes and a hand up your skirt. Love's listening to some berk telling you about Aston Villa and road holding in the rain, then cleaning up five pints of beer vomit off your dress. That's love. [*She begins to cry.* **Alberto** *goes to her but she pushes him off violently*] Take your hands off me. Two-timing sod. I know about you. Does Ali? Yeah — this one here, old smoothy chops here — don't look like a married man, does he . . . he's got three kids in Figueras! [*Pause*] I heard.

[*Silence*]

Ali: Is that true, Alberto?

Alberto: Yes . . . it is true. Problems with my wife, but this is Spain — so she must stay my wife. I love my children, though.

Ali: Then how can you leave them every summer?

Alberto: Because it is best . . . there is the most money here. . . .

[*Pause*]

Ali: I'd like to see them.

Alberto: What?

Ali: Your children. . . . I'd like to see them.

[*Pause*]

Alberto: I borrow José's car . . . we go tomorrow . . . there is a *fiesta* and so I must go. . . . You come.

[*He goes, she follows. Now* **Rick** *is alone with* **Lynne** *and* **Karen**]

Rick: Dry your eyes. Here. [*Hands her a handkerchief*]

Lynne: Tar. [*She blows her nose very loudly*] Sound like a bloody tugboat, don't I? Wish I could be ladylike. Like you Karen. You smoke a bloody cigar and look ladylike and grand. If I smoked a cigar I'd look like Lew Grade on a bad day. [*She wipes her eyes*] Great smell this . . . Aqua Lavender. Took some of that home with me last year . . . put it on me sheets . . . made me think of him. . . . Christ he's a lousy sod and I can't hate him. Gotta fag?

Karen: Here.

Lynne: Be glad to get home for a decent English snout.

Karen: I thought you were having a real good time.

Lynne: Real . . . good . . . time. What's real? Me mam says to me – men are all sods. Hated her for that. Loved me dad. Night of the accident . . . had this nightmare – premonition. That's how much I loved him. Used to wait outside the boozer for him – me a kid, drawers hanging down round me knees and he'd come out with a bag of crisps and a glass of lemonade and he'd pour a drop of his beer in it and I thought great! Shandy, I'm only eight. But she was right, me mam, I see it now. That's all men do – buy you a drink so's they can keep you quiet while they do what they want. That's it. That's real.

Karen: Doesn't have to be like that. You make it how you want it.

Lynne: You're all right. You've got brains. You're clever. They last. You've either got to have brains or look sexy. And if you look good – cash in while it lasts. There's fifty years of washing dishes and that waiting.

[*Al shouts from offstage*]

Al: Coming to Fat Cat's, sexy?

Lynne: OK, Al. You've seduced me with your glittering chat. [*To* **Karen**] Only two nights to go — don't waste a minute, eh?

[*She goes off with* **Al**. *Roars are heard. Pause*]

Karen: What did your mam used to say to you?

Rick: Old Cockney lady. She used to say — if you ain't in bed by ten o'clock — come home. She used to say to me, write your letters slowly, son — I'm not a very fast reader.

Karen: You went away from her, then?

Rick: When things got bad . . . I went away.

Karen: Old habits die hard.

Rick: Maybe.

Karen: And do you get away from the things you're running away from?

Rick: You're on holiday . . . no heavy conversations.

Karen: In your villa . . . photos of a woman. [*Pause*] She looks like me.

Rick: I. . . .

Karen: What?

Rick: Yeah, you do look like her. Like she used to look.

Karen: Is she—?

Rick: I don't know where she is now. I met her first time at the Playboy Club. She was . . . irresistible. I'd made a little packet with me motoryard. Me own boss. Three mechanics working for me . . . business was getting better and better. I felt . . . over the moon. And then Pam, on top. It was too much. She was taking me for a ride . . . milking me. I didn't care. I wanted her. Then after a bit the other guys put me wise about her. She was just taking the micky. I got tanked up. Pulled another bint. A sweet thing. From Bradford. Had me

Cadillac. Taking her home. It was raining. The Bayswater Road like a skid pan. I don't know where the other car came from. There was no time to hit the anchors. I was too smashed. Next minute I'm standing in the rain hysterical and this kid . . . from Bradford in her thin dress and scented hair is a pile of bones and blood suspended from the windscreen. [*Pause*] I got two years. I should have had ten. They should have strung me up. When I got out, the business was gone. Me deputy manager had sold all the motors and run up five grand of debts. I come here. Someone told me keeping fit might help . . . to forget. I did Canadian Airman's exercises, I run up hills. Then I found the bottle again. . . . I found. . . . I dunno.

Karen: And the sun makes things better?

Rick: It makes them . . . not so bad.

Karen: And in the winter?

Rick: They're cold winters, sometimes. It's quiet.

Karen: Sometimes, there's snow.

Rick: I dunno.

Karen: My grandfather said there was thick snow.

Rick: I've never heard you mention your family before.

Karen: They're dead. . . . I don't know much about my mother . . . my father. An uncle showed me my grandfather's letters. . . . I got to know him, I think, through his letters. . . . He came here with the Brigade . . . a romantic, a Lansbury socialist. . . . I wanted to . . . find the object of his obsession. I wanted to see the places he wrote about.

Rick: On a hundred quid package tour?

Karen: It's all I could afford . . . his grave must be up there somewhere, up in these rolling hills, on that bleak plateau. . . . In the shadow of a tree, I hope. Anonymous and out of the sun. I'd like to carve . . . some memento.

Rick: Such as?

Karen: His last letter, postmarked Madrid, 26 March . . . two
days before it fell. . . . Madrid was the last city to fall to
Franco, three years and a million lives after it all started.
. . . Sense of futility in his letter. The inevitable looming and
yet . . . an assessment, personal . . . it would make a good
gravestone message. . . . His own obituary, very simple pencil
on yellowing paper: lived a life, planted a flower, sat in the sun,
ate, drunk, made love . . . lived a life.

[*Long pause*]

Rick: It's getting cold, Karen.

Karen: Yes. . . .

[*They go and the lights fade. Music: Jim Capaldi,* Love Hurts]

Scene: **The patio** – day time. *A couple of girls are sunbathing.*
Tony, Sid, Steve *and* **Al** *mime bullfighting.* **Sid** *brandishes ban-
derillas and pokes the girls with them.*

Tony: I'm going to take this up when I get home. Epping
Forest, Saturday afternoons, scaring the tripes out of the cows.

Al: I felt sorry for those poor horses, really cruel.

Sid: They love it.

Al: Getting their sides torn out?

Sid: Like showjumping. See the horse crash over the fence on
its plums and the rider says [*Posh voice*] 'Nonsense, old chap,
the horses love it.'

Al: I haven't had a bet for a fortnight.

Tony: You clown – there's a William Hill's on the *promenada*
next to the chip shop.

Al: Now he tells me! Last day here, and—

[**Tony** *goes and the other lads loll.* **Lynne** *enters with a* **Waiter** *who begins to massage her after they have both sat down*]

Waiter: You like that?

Lynne: If I didn't I'd put you in a half nelson.

Waiter: Tonight, we go for a walk?

Lynne: Why walk, when cabs are dirt cheap?

[**Helen** *enters*]

Helen: There you are.

Lynne: What's up with you? Looked like you've dropped your charm bracelet down a shower plughole.

Helen: I'm so sad . . . last day . . . I could stay here forever.

Lynne: Lose yer passport. Oh, do that again, Henrique, that's lovely. What's up with twinkle fingers?

Helen: They're practising 'The Last Waltz.' They have to play it tonight and they all hate it.

Lynne: Hey, Henrique – get us some drinks, eh?

Waiter: No money.

Lynne: On tick. I'll barter me sunhat to pay.

Helen: I wish Dave hadn't sent that telegram. Lousy thing to do. Just forgotten about him and really enjoying myself. . . .

Lynne: Could have been worse, he could have turned up.

Helen: What do you think of Rod? I mean compared to Dave? You know them both.

Lynne: Aye, but not that well. It's what you want, in't it love. Only you can decide. Dave's secure and reliable. Rod'll lead you a hell of a dance, but maybe you like dancing. It's stodge and filling – or going hungry and the occasional oysters.

Helen: It always ends up with bloody food with you.

Lynne: There's a sparkle in your eyes, kid. Dave never put a sparkle in your eyes.

[**Karen** *enters carrying books*]

Lynne: Hi, you scribbler.

Karen: Hi.

Lynne: Where did you go today? To see the daleks or Doctor Who's telephone box?

Karen: Why have you got that towel all over you?

Lynne: I'm trying to just tan me hand where the bandage was. Get that hand the same colour as the rest of me. Christ — One hundred twenty quid this holiday — and I go back with me hand looking like I'm wearing a bleeding bridesmaid's glove.

[**Ali** *enters crying. They all look at her*]

Karen: What's the matter, love?

Ali: I . . . I . . . I. . . .

[*Pause*]

Karen: What is it?

Ali: I saw Alberto's wife. [*She howls*]

Lynne: Bloody hell — she must be ugly. Terrify you, did she?

Ali: Noooo. No it wasn't like that. He took me to his village There was a *fiesta*. It was beautiful. The whole village was a blaze of coloured flags and flowers and there were clowns and dancers and fire-eaters and all the children in the village dressed up in their white communion clothes looking so beautiful. And me and Alberto were standing there . . . and I felt this little girl, she could only have been four or maybe younger . . . tugging at Alberto's trousers and he looked down and she said . . . 'Papa' . . . and hugged his legs and cried and . . . we looked, and there were two other of his children standing there looking at us . . . I felt so . . . dirty and disgusting and . . . then I saw this woman . . . all dressed in old, dark clothes . . . face almost white and great dark rings around her eyes, no expression but . . . the way she was looking at me. . . . I knew she was his wife. . . . I never ever want to be looked at by a woman like that again . . . I come back on the train by myself. I feel like I don't know I could feel so ashamed and bad. . . .

[*A pause as the lads gather round to look at* Ali. *She continues to cry*]

[Alberto *enters, looking worried. They all look at him*]

Alberto: Ali, please. I don't know what to say.

[*They all circle him.* Al *leaps forward and forces* Alberto *to the ground.* Alberto *groans as the others put in the boot. The* Girls *scream 'No!' etc. Suddenly* Waiters *appear from everywhere and join in the fight. The* Girls *continue to scream. The* Guardia *arrive with police horns and whistles sounding. Pandemonium. The English lads are badly beaten, arrested protesting, and led off. The* Girls *follow shouting after them*]

Scene: Leaving. *As the lights come up,* Waiters *are arranging suitcases and various luggage.* Girls *are crying, with their arms around* Waiters *who hand them their suitcases.* Rick *watches.* Tony *enters.*

Tony: Here, Rick what's going to happen to them, then?

Rick: They're not going home today, that's for sure.

Tony: Way I heard it, the waiters did them over good and proper. Bit out of order bunging the lads in jail — they'd already got beaten up.

Rick: They did it once too often.

Tony: What'll happen, then?

Rick: Spanish courts can take a long time to deal with matters like this. The British Consul is doing his best. But it happens so often I think he's less than dedicated to a swift release. Just count yourself lucky you were out of it.

Tony: Going to be bloody nice this, in't it. Going home — the only bloke on a plane load of bints. . . . [*He laughs*] Yeah, bloody nice. Oh well, this time Monday in the bakery. I never wake up till after eleven.

Rick: I thought bakers started work at the crack of dawn.

Tony: Yeah, that's when I start work, but I don't wake up till after eleven. [**Rick** *laughs*] Don't know what I'll tell their mums.

Rick: Perhaps a week, they'll be back home. I hope you learned a lesson.

Tony: Well, Mac, see you next year?

[*He picks up his case and joins the* **Girls** *with the* **Waiters**. **Lynne** *enters with a* **Waiter**]

Lynne: And if you ever happen to be passing Hull, do drop in for a cup of tea.

Waiter: The minute the season is over, I come to you.

Lynne: Yeah, I've heard that before — oo, you are lovely.

[*She hugs him.* **Peter** *enters*]

Peter: Well, girls, I hope you all enjoyed yourselves.

Girls: Rubbish.

Peter: And tell the lads — I hope next year *none of them come back.*

Girls: Oi, oi.

Jan: Peter, can we take a picture of you?

Peter: Oh, well, yes, why not?

Tony: Back a bit, Pete, back a bit.

Paula: Just a bit more—

Lynne: So I can get you all in — all your magnificent body — back just another yard.

[*He topples over the wall into the pool with a loud splash. Roars of delight. The coach horn sounds. The* **Girls** *leave, accompanied by* **Waiters**. **Rod** *and* **Helen**, *who is crying, enter*]

Helen: Well. . . .

Rod: Yeah.

Helen: Never forget you, I won't. Never.

Rod: Good.

Helen: I've never known no one like you. Well, I'd better get going then. . . .

Rod: Hey — give us your phone number. . . .

Helen: Only if you really want it.

Rod: I do.

Helen: Are you sure?

Rod: I wouldn't say I want it if I didn't want it.

Helen: I think you're just saying you want it because you think I want you to ask for it, but. . . .

Rod: Can I please have your phone number?

Helen: You really want it?

Rod: I really want it.

Helen: All right then. . . . Oh. . . .

Rod: What?

Helen: I'm not on the phone.

Rod: Christ.

Helen: At home I mean. I am at work, but they don't like us to have personal calls at Whitworth and Company.

Rod: Take a risk — be bold. Give us it.

Helen: All right then. Here. [*She writes it down*] I don't . . . don't know what I'm going to do about Dave . . . don't know how I'll feel when I see him again. . . .

Rod: Stay cool. It's your life.

Helen: I know it is. That's what worries me to death. The responsibility of having to be in charge of it. I come here two weeks ago all tensed up . . . and all all those worries went away. . . . I didn't think about work or Dave — well, not much . . . and, going back now — and all the worries are crowding in again. [**Ali** *enters*] How do you feel?

Ali: Very different to the person who come. I'm never going to talk to a married man again. Next bloke I like, I'll phone up Somerset House in London to make sure he's not married.

Helen: We'd better get going, then. . . .

Ali: Oh well! — back to the land of elevenses. Eight coffees — three with —

Helen: Two without, one black with.

Lynne: Two without, one with lemon, four Danish pastries and—

Lynne/Helen/Ali: A Bovril for old Jock!

Ali: Maybe they've taken on a new girl — a junior. Maybe when I get back I'll not have to do it anymore.

Lynne: That coach is getting full. I want to sit at the back, be the last one to leave.

Ali: I hope the plane doesn't make your ears go funny.

Helen: Pardon?

[*They laugh as they leave. All have gone except* **Rick** *and* **Rod. Karen** *enters, carrying a small case. Pause*]

Rick: I hope you have a good flight. No cloud. You'll see a lot of Spain.

Karen: Maybe.

Rick: Well, *adíos.*

Karen: *Adíos.*

Rick: Will I see you next summer?

Karen: I doubt it. Good-bye, Rick. It's been good knowing you.
[*She goes. Pause*]

Rod: Do you think she'll finish her novel?

Rick: Maybe. But I tell you one thing . . . there won't be many laughs in it.

Rod: Shall we have a drink?

Rick: You set them up. I'll just see the coach off.

[**Rod** *enters the bar.* **Rick** *raises his hat and waves at the sound of the coach departing. Silence. He slowly returns to the hotel. Music:* Here Comes the Sun. *The lights fade*]

The End

Follow-up Activities

Some Enchanted Evening

Discussion

Which do you think is the right job for Peter? What advice would you give him — about his job? About Sue? And about the lass?

What sort of pressures do Peter's father and mother put on him?

And how does Sue 'pressure' him? Do any of them think about what is really best for him? Should we try to influence the lives of our relations and friends?

In what ways are Peter's mother and Sue alike? How would you defend Sue?

Do you think Peter will be happy with the lass? Is she the sort of girl Sue predicts he will end up with?

Do you think that it is usually the girl who leads the boy into marriage?

Do you think the playwright is 'fair' in the way he presents the women in his play? Why — or why not?

What sort of person is the television reporter? How much of what he says do you agree with?

In which parts is this a very realistic play, and where is it exaggerated?

Peter's father says (page 00) 'People aren't *made* to be free.' Do you agree? Do you think people are meant to be happy?

What advice about your own career or future do you get from this play?

Improvisation

Improvise scenes in which the minor characters in the play report the incidents on the bridge (as they have seen them) to friends and colleagues.

Improvise the interviews the television reporter might record with the various people present.

Plan, rehearse and stage his 'report' on the incident, complete with 'clips' from his interview.

Devise a 'This Is Your Life' programme with Peter as the central character.

Plan, rehearse and present a 'This Is Your Life' programme about someone you know, or about a character from another play or novel.

Improvise realistic scenes between a 'genuine' potential suicide, the people he or she knows, and a Samaritan.

Improvise either a serious or an exaggerated play in which the central character (a schoolboy or girl) is nagged at from all sides, i.e. by friends, family, teachers.

Improvise scenes in which the traditional male/female roles are reversed: for example, ones in which a girl sees her shy boyfriend home, late at night; or ones in a saloon bar in the American West where cowgirls fight out their quarrels to the distress of the barboy or the other frightened men present.

Writing

Write of a time when you have been treated as though you were much younger than you really were, or when other people [possibly parents or maybe friends] have 'fought' over you or shown they were jealous about you.

Describe a time when you felt let down by someone's lack of interest in your worries or success.

Write a comic monologue describing a day in which everyone 'got at you'. Don't be afraid to exaggerate a bit, but keep it within the bounds of credibility or it will fail to be comic and become merely silly.

Write a script for a 'This Is Your Life' programme about yourself that might be shown now, or one that might be shown in forty years' time.

Write up as short stories or playscripts some of the scenes you have improvised while working on this play.

The Filleting Machine

Discussion

What are Davy's reasons for not wanting to work in the Town Clerk's office, and for wanting to work on the fish quay?

What similar arguments might occur in a year or so about Alice? Why?

Why does Davy's mother want him to work in an office? Do you agree with her? Does she want what is right for Davy? Is she a loving mother? Just what are the problems she faces in life?

Is Davy's father a likeable man? Is he a good father? For what would you criticize him? How would you defend him?

Who is the stronger character, Ma or Da? How do they regard each other?

Which job will Davy do? Why? Do you think the filleting machine will alter things?

What will happen to Alice?

What arguments do you have about your own future? How will you decide which job you will take, if you have a choice? What do you want from your job? What is a 'good' job?

Do you want to 'get on'? Is it wrong to waste your talents? Not to use your brains or skills?

Will you want your children to do better than you do? What must be the problems facing a parent when their children start thinking about work?

Improvisation

Improvise scenes that might take place some months later:

a)   with Davy working in the Town Clerk's office
b)   with Davy working on the fish quay and liking his work
c)   with Davy working on the fish quay and regretting his
      decision.

(What difference to these scenes will it make if Da is in or out
of work?)

Improvise a play with Alice as the central character.

Create a series of scenes and then develop them into a documentary or a play about choosing a job. You could include scenes
between school or college leavers and their careers teachers (with
the teacher either trying to persuade the young person to be
'realistic' or to be more ambitious): between parents and careers
teachers, and between parents and children.

Improvise a play about a family in which some members (like
Ma in this play) believe things can be changed, and others believe
everything will always be the same.

Writing

Write a story about Davy or Alice starting work, from their
point of view, or from Ma's or Da's viewpoint.

Describe an argument or discussion you have had about
your own future.

Describe the sorts of jobs you would and would not like, and
try to say why.

Write a story or playscript about a meal-time with a family
you have created in one of your improvisations.

Annie Kenney

Discussion

Which of the characters do we care about? Why?

Exactly what were the injustices or problems that the Suffragette Movement was fighting?

What progress do its members make in this play? What are their precise achievements?

How do the members of the Pankhurst family [Mrs Pankhurst and her daughters Christabel and Sylvia] differ from each other?

How does Annie regard them? How do they treat her? Does their difference in class play any part in the story?

What problems have you encountered or observed that were the result of class differences (or differences in wealth or poverty)? Are such differences important? Do people take them seriously? In what ways?

Do you think that it is the middle class that 'gets things done'? In what ways is this play as much about the struggles of the workers to have a say in politics as it is about the Suffragette Movement?

This play was televised in a series which had the sub-title 'A Gentle Rebellion'. In what ways was it a gentle rebellion? In later years Sylvia Pankhurst described the Movement as 'too eccentric' and 'too privileged'. What do you think she meant? Do you agree?

How does the present-day 'women's lib' movement compare with the Suffragette Movement? What are your thoughts on the issue?

Are violent demonstrations ever justified?

At elections, does it matter whether those entitled to vote do so?

Improvisation

Suppose radio or television programmes existed at the time of these events. Improvise the interviews, reports and programmes that might have been shown after the various public meetings that are included in the play.

Improvise your own version of this story or of a topic you have studied recently in your History course.

Decide on an issue which you feel strongly about, such as greater rights or freedom for a particular group of people, or a situation which you feel is unjust. Improvise meetings at which a group of supporters of the cause encourage others to join them; a meeting between the leaders of the group and their opponents; committee meetings to further the cause and to plan a campaign. Finally, hold a 'public' meeting to explain the matter.

Writing

Write the diary that Annie Kenney [or one of the other characters] might have kept during the events covered by the play.

In real life, many of the characters portrayed in the play must have written letters in order to keep each other informed of events. Decide who might have written such letters, and to whom; then write the letters you think they may have sent.

Write newspaper accounts that might have appeared after the two public meetings included in the play.

Write the story of a campaign you have observed or been involved in.

Research, plan, write, rehearse and present your own documentary play (see page 16).

Here Comes the Sun

Discussion

Which of the characters do you like or care about? Why? Which do you dislike? Why? Are there any you admire?

How do the English girls differ from each other?

Why has each of them come to Spain? What is each hoping to get out of the holiday? Why are Rick and Rod there?

Many of them have a 'weak spot'; they are vulnerable in some way. What 'weak spots' can you see in them?

How do you think they might remember this holiday? Is it a success?

What do you expect of a holiday? What would be your ideal holiday?

Why do you think some people automatically dislike people of another nationality? How do you regard foreigners?

Do different 'rules' apply to our behaviour when we are away from home? If so, does this matter?

What rules do you think should apply to young people about the consumption of alcohol?

What do you think are some of the causes of violence and vandalism (both in the play and in real life)?

In what ways is this a sad or pessimistic play?

Improvisation

In pairs, improvise conversations that the various characters might have on the flight home, about the holiday and about work.

In groups, improvise conversations the characters might have about the holiday with workmates and friends who did not go on the holiday.

Select one of the characters and improvise the scene in that character's home, when he or she returns from the holiday and is asked all about it by parents and other relatives.

Improvise (in English!) the conversations the Spaniards might have about this and other groups of English holidaymakers.

Plan and act out television commercials for supposedly exotic holidays and resorts, and then improvise scenes showing 'reality'.

Make up your own play about a school trip or holiday (possibly an educational cruise or other trip abroad).

Improvise a play called 'Here Comes the Rain' about a group of young foreigners on holiday in Britain.

Writing

Write a selection of the postcards and letters the group might have sent home.

Collect together a selection of package holiday brochures and (after studying them) write a description of the sort of holiday you might expect from a particular 'package'. Try to decide which of the holidays would offer the best value.

Describe a holiday you've been on that proved memorable in some way (either because everything went well or badly); or describe what would be your ideal holiday.

Write a true story about an outbreak of violence or vandalism you have seen, and which proved particularly silly or mindless, or which got out of hand.

A story called 'The Foreigner'.